le You Will Need

14/10/23

This is a note from the author.

You are holding a very first copy of my book dedicated to interview preperation.

As the author, I am delighted to donate it to Oxfam Bookshop, and I hope it finds its way into your hands.

I put my heart and soul into creating this book, and I hope it proves to be a valuable resource for you on your interview journey.

If you find it helpful, consider visiting my blog at www.myrto.substack.com for more insights and updates.

This book has undergone edits and improvements, but this copy holds a special place as one of the very first.

Best of luck with your interview preperation

Myrto xx

To my younger self, who navigated the maze of interviews,
with curiosity and determination, this is a testament to our
journey.
To my mentors, who saw potential where I saw doubt,
your guidance has been my north star.
To the upcoming generation, may you find your unique path,
and know that each challenge is a step towards your dream.
To my family, who provided wings to my aspirations.
and roots to my values, your unwavering support has been my
fortress.
And my partner, the wind beneath my wings,
thank you for supporting my vision to grow by helping others grow.

This book is a tribute to all of you.

Table of Contents

Hi There! Let's Get Acquainted...........................1
Front Row Seats, Navigating Interviews with
Confidence 3
Getting the Mindset Right 5
Re-defining the 'Successful Interview' 11
Decoding the Interview Outcome 18
Interview Preparation.......................................24
    Understanding the Key Elements....................24
    Telephone Interview-Screening with a Recruiter
   27
    Competency-Based/ Behavioural Interview 29
    Case Study 33
    Assessment Centre..44
    Online Interview..49
    Master Your Elevator Pitch 51
    Identify Your Top 3 Challenges and
    Achievements...54
    Prepare Your Questions for the interviewer(s) 54
Unlocking Insights 57
    Leveraging Online Platforms and AI for
    Interview Success 57
    LinkedIn 57
    Glassdoor...58
    ChatGPT...60
Recognize Your Personality Traits.....................62
The Interview Day...65
Post Interview Self-Reflection 68
The Power of the 'Thank You' Note 72
Waiting to Hear Back 74
Managing Interview Outcome 77
    Receiving a job offer 77
    Handling an offer when expecting another one79

No offer 81
A Parting Note on Owning Your Interview Journey
.... 84
Appendix 86
   Online Networking Templates 86
   Post Interview 'Thank you' Email Templates .. 89
   Approaching Competency Based and Behavioural
   Questions 92
   Questions for the interviewers 126

The Only Interview Guide You Will Need

Lessons I wish I had early on

Hi There! Let's Get Acquainted

I'm Myrto, and if you're holding this book, it means you're already on the way to making some waves. After bagging my Master's at the University of Manchester (Go Mancunians!), I jumped headfirst into the ever-evolving world of HR. From the thrilling lanes of Recruitment and HR Tech to the game-changing worlds of Product Management and Transformation, I've been there, done that, and got some swanky titles to show for it.

Here's the tea: I'm lowkey obsessed with mentoring and championing young visionaries like you. We're talking about turning those sweaty-palm, heart-racing interviews into your very own rock concerts. And that's exactly why I've packed all my adventures, along with some golden nuggets from my own mentors, into these pages for you.

Consider me your cheerleader, on this roller-coaster ride of your early career. I will be sharing with you of insights to elevate your interview game and help you discover, that superpower potential within you.

Real talk: A winning mindset? That's the real MVP. Let's redefine the interview game, finding those moments of personal growth and unearthing those transformative experiences that are so much more than just "did I get the job?". Think of interviews as your backstage passes to learning, growing, and crafting your unique path to awesomeness.

Whether you're fresh out of the academic oven or hitting that restart button on your career, I'm here, ready with all the tools and glitter to help you shine brighter than ever. Let's turn those interviews from nerve-wracking auditions into your headline shows.

So, strap in and get comfy. We will be making a short journey to interview-land. By the end of this book, you will be equipped with a trophy; your own magic wand to ace interviews and shape your career with confidence and a higher level of awareness.

Front Row Seats, Navigating Interviews with Confidence

Flashback to me, fresh out of uni in the UK, buzzing with excitement and a mixtape of jitters about my first-ever job interviews. Degree? Check. An impressive-ish resume? Yep. But little did I know, I was about to kick off an epic quest, discovering both the '9 to 5' realm and, well... myself.

The early levels? Bit of a mixed bag. Sometimes, I would fumble through interview questions, or throw out ending questions that were, let's just say, not my greatest hits. There were times I felt like I smashed it, even got those instant dopamine hits of on-the-spot praises, but still, no "Welcome to the team!" emails in my inbox.

Being ghosted or getting that "thanks, but no thanks" reply? Trust me, it was a whole mood, especially when I felt like I was this close. The mental replay of "Where did I go wrong?" was on a constant loop.

Fast-forward a decade and change, and here I am, having levelled up in the game of life. From jobs that felt like epic wins to others that were... well, 'character-building'. From bosses that pushed my buttons to some that I totally pushed back. The journey? A rollercoaster of learnings, with more plot twists and turns yet to come.

Peeping my early avatar, I see a player who could've used a few cheat codes, been more zen, more 'in the groove'. I realize now that scoring a job wasn't just about having mad skills or the flashiest achievements. Oh, how I wish I could send my present-day wisdom back to younger me via some time-traveling DMs! But, time machines aren't on Amazon (yet), so I'll do the next best thing.

Enter this book: A compilation of my levels, Easter eggs, and (yes) epic fails. My goal? To guild you up and get you bossing those interviews with all the swagger and smarts.

So, if interviews have ever left you feeling like you're navigating a maze blindfolded, or if you've ever felt that mid-game anxiety, know this: You've got company. Let's co-op this challenge, level up from my past glitches, and gear up to slay any interview boss battles that come our way.

Getting the Mindset Right

Establishing the right mindset is crucial when it comes to approaching an interview opportunity. In fact, it might be the most important factor in determining a successful outcome. An interview invitation is more than just a chance to showcase your skills; it's a unique opportunity to connect with individuals within a company you aspire to join. These connections can prove invaluable, extending far beyond the confines of the interview process.

I've noticed that many candidates experience anxiety and excessive worry leading up to an interview. While it's natural to feel a certain level of nervousness, unchecked anxiety can hinder your ability to shine and present your best self. It's essential to remember that stress can manifest in your tone of voice and posture, impacting how you are perceived by recruiters and hiring managers.

Keep in mind, that the interviewers are not only evaluating your skills, but also assessing your personality. Therefore, it's crucial to exude confidence, even if you don't meet every requirement of the job description. The interview is your opportunity to convince others that you are the ideal candidate. In order to do so effectively, you are the one to believe in yourself first.

For candidates looking for a confidence boost before an interview, I offer the following advice.

It's okay not to tick all the boxes

Understand that you don't need to meet every single requirement of the job description. No candidate does. Having around 70-80% of the necessary skills and qualifications is often sufficient. If you met very closely every single of the expected and desired skills and were perfect in every aspect for this role, there would be limited room for growth and development in the role, which is a risk as potentially can lead to boredom. Recruiters are aware that hiring "unicorns" is unrealistic, and they understand that candidates have areas for growth. As long as you demonstrate enthusiasm, a willingness to learn and develop, and an awareness of the areas you need to focus on for growth, you'll be in good shape. Demonstrating awareness of points that may be proven challenging to you, and having an idea of how we can tackle them, is essentially the best sign of confidence and self-awareness, that any recruiter and hiring manager would expect and love to see.

You need to believe in yourself first

Cultivate confidence in your abilities and demonstrate certainty that you want and can excel in the role. Being aware of the areas where you may lack experience and showing a proactive mindset in addressing them is a sign of confidence. Avoid attempting to cover up gaps in your experience, as it can come across as lack of authenticity. Recruiters and hiring managers can easily detect when candidates are not being truthful based on the examples they provide. My best advice is to be genuine, be yourself, and convince yourself first why you want and are capable of performing the job.

Confidence, a calm demeanour and authenticity are the keys to having a meaningful conversation that flows naturally during an interview, which is ultimately the goal. Before the interview, take a moment to reflect on your experiences, both personal and professional, and consider three of your biggest achievements you have overcome, as well three of your biggest accomplishments. This reflection will help you be equipped with strong and genuine examples that you can easily adjust to most type of competency-based interviews.

Become aware of your strengths

To increase your confidence, consider asking for feedback from those who know you well, such as colleagues, classmates, or professors. You may be pleasantly surprised by the positive qualities and strengths they recognize in you. If you're unsure how to initiate feedback requests, an effective approach is the "SKS" model: ask others what you should Stop doing, what you should Keep doing, and what you should Start doing. More simply, you can ask what your strong qualities are and where you could focus to become a more valuable colleague, friend, student, or professional (depending on the relationship you have with the other person). You can ask feedback in person or in writing (via email or survey). Whatever you choose to do, it may always be good to allow people time to think and reflect, before sharing and not ask them on the spot, so you can ensure they provide you with good insights.

Trust me, you will be very surprised with what you will hear. This exercise is proven to be very beneficial as a confidence boost as well as the employee's development. I did a similar exercise with a former line manager of mine, as part of an internal corporate coaching program. Having my line manager share openly feedback about me with my coach, was an eye-opening activity, especially for my confidence. I was pleased to hear so many positive things, that I took for granted about myself. We as people tend to focus on our weaknesses and may be undervaluing our key strengths and the value we add for others.

Another way to feel more aware of your strengths could be taking a strengths assessment online. There's plenty available online, some are free and some at have a small cost associated but could be worth it if you are interested to learn more about yourself.

One example is Gallup's Clifton Strengths assessment, which helps identify your unique strengths and areas where you naturally excel. By providing personalized insights into your behaviour and thinking, it guides your focus on enhancing those strengths rather than fixing weaknesses. This not only boosts your self-confidence but also aids in understanding how you can contribute to a team and prepare effectively for interviews. It's a valuable tool for aligning your career goals with what you do best, making you stand out in the job market.

There are also other free strength assessments available that could offer valuable insights. I list some of these below.

- 16Personalities: Based on the Myers-Briggs Type Indicator, this test provides insight into your personality type and how it influences your career choices.

- VIA Character Strengths Survey: This tool identifies your top character strengths, helping you understand what motivates you and where you might excel in the workplace.

- Holland Code (RIASEC) Test: This assessment aligns your interests with potential career paths, helping you identify roles that could be a good fit for your personality and preferences.

These tests can be a great starting point for self-discovery and career planning, helping you and your fellow graduates navigate the job market with greater confidence and direction.

Know that they already like you

The fact that you received an interview invitation means that your profile stood out and they are genuinely interested in meeting you. So, worry less about your background and focus more on preparing for the interview, practicing your responses, and researching the company to ensure you stand out among other candidates.

Trust me, I've been there, and chances are, so have most people who have a job. The journey of anxiety and pain until landing your first or desired job is one shared by many. In the following sections, I'll provide tips and best practices for approaching upcoming interviews that can significantly impact your interview journey and future career progression.

Re-defining the 'Successful Interview'

When we think of interviews, it's natural to focus on the end result: landing the job offer. But let's shift our perspective and reshape our understanding of a 'successful interview.' It's not just about the outcome; it's about the valuable learnings, reflections, and insights we gain, fostering a growth mindset and building connections. So, buckle up and let's dive into what truly defines a successful interview.

Feedback - A Gift to Propel Your Growth

Imagine receiving feedback that gives you a clear picture of how you performed, how you came across, and what impressed the interviewers. It's like holding a map to navigate your future interviews with confidence. Feedback is a priceless gift, an indicator of your strengths and areas for improvement based on the interviewer's expectations.

And even if feedback isn't offered initially, don't hesitate to ask for it. It's not petty; it's critical. Soak up the insights and let them propel you to the next level in future interviews.

If feedback is not provided following an interview, even after asking for it, don't take this to heart. I personally consider providing candidates with feedback, after they have invested time to prepare and show up for an interview is expected and is a way of demonstrating appreciation and respect towards them. Companies that don't share feedback with candidates following an interview, especially upon candidate's request, mot likely have large volume of applications and or a not efficient way of recruitment tracking. The way you are treated during an interview process regardless of the final outcome, is one of the most reflective ways of a company's values and culture.

Self-Reflection - The Power of Your Own Insights

After the end of the interview, even before hearing feedback from the interviewer, take a moment for self-reflection. Think, how did you feel during the interview? Did you exude confidence and comfort, while answering questions? Reflect on any challenging questions and consider how you could have tackled them better. And guess what? The internet, with its vast resources, can be your trusty sidekick. Research the best approaches to tricky questions, equip yourself, and emerge stronger for future encounters. Embrace self-reflection as a personal growth tool on your interview journey.

The first thing I used to do after my interviews those early days, would be to reflect on how I answered the questions. If there were any particular questions, I came across for the first time and felt uncertain on the best approach to respond, like for example, ''Where do you see yourself in the next 5 years?" I used to search online to see what the best answers to this questions would be, and what someone should cover and avoid saying. I would then assess my response against the results of my research. This approach helped me improve my interview technique, and respond to questions in a smarter way.

Luckily now technology is much more advanced compared to 10 years ago. With the latest developments in Artificial Intelligence (AI), early careers have now even further power and tools to help themselves navigate successfully the interview preparation processes, understand what questions are being asked during interviews and what are the best ways of answering these questions. Take for example ChatGPT, which is an AI tool. With the right prompts, ChatGPT can help candidates understand frequently asked questions in particular companies or industries for roles. Apart from helping you come up with a list of possible questions you may be asked for a particular role, ChatGPT can also help you find out what are the best ways to answer and structure these questions in an interview. You could even relate to this, as having a free interview coach supporting you.

Industry Insights - Unlocking the Secrets of Success

During an interview, you may notice that the hiring manager may often share insights about their team, current or upcoming projects, as well as key the skills they seeking for. This insider knowledge is like a treasure chest of industry insights, providing a deeper understanding of sector needs and crucial skills.

It's a sneak peek into the world you aspire to join, empowering you to align your aspirations with the demands of the field. So, absorb these insights like a sponge, and let them shape your critical thinking as you navigate your career and any future interviews.

Company Culture Insights - Where You Truly Belong

Beyond industry insights, an interview offers a unique window into a company's culture. It's a chance to gauge if the organization aligns with your values and if you can picture yourself thriving there.

Observe the interviewers' approach, the atmosphere, and the people around you. Do they radiate happiness or stress? Trust your instincts and reflect on whether this is a place where you can truly flourish and find fulfilment.

And remember, even virtual interviews can offer glimpses into company culture through conversations with interviewers, as well as how you are treated through the whole interview process. For example, a well organised company with values of respect towards its employee's will ensure that candidates are informed of next steps of the process and have prompt sense communication. In the contrary, if the people you encounter are stressed, seem tired or under pressure, then this could be a possible indication of a stressful and overloaded working environment.

Gain Interview Insights for Life - Unlocking Your Potential

Every interview experience brings you closer to mastery. You encounter various interview techniques, questions, and case studies, adding powerful tools to your arsenal. These insights extend beyond a single job opportunity; they equip you for future interviews and pave the way for your professional growth. Whether you aspire to become a line manager at some point in your career, or simply want to refine your interviewing skills, embrace the lessons that interviews teach you. Your journey as an interviewee has the power to transform you into a confident, skilled evaluator of talent.

From my own journey, only from the exposure I got from the different interviews I attended as a graduate, I gained insights that helped me, not only to improve my interview technique, but also apply my takeaways and influence and coordinate recruitment processes on my own, coaching Managers and Directors on best practices of interview processes, communications, and selection. My interview experience as a candidate helped me apply knowledge on the job, through the first steps of my career.

Building Bridges - Your Professional Network Awaits

An interview is not just a transaction, it's an opportunity to build meaningful connections. From recruiters to interviewers and hiring managers, you encounter professionals, who can open doors to exciting prospects.

Make a lasting impression, nurture those connections, and expand your professional network. Even if you don't secure the job, don't underestimate the power of personal feedback, advice, or future opportunities that may arise through these connections. Your network is a valuable asset, and interviews are the gateway to expanding it.

Gather Insights for the Journey Ahead

As you go through interviews and observe different interview styles and techniques, you will notice that you will start becoming familiar with common and uncommon practices. Over time, you will develop a keen sense of interview dynamics, enabling you to navigate future encounters with flair.

These insights will prepare you, not just your short-term goal of securing a job, but also for long-term career progression. You never know when you might find yourself on the other side of the table, conducting interviews and guiding others based on the wisdom you've gained.

So, remember this: every interview is an opportunity for growth, no matter the outcome. Embrace the journey, savour the learnings, and let each experience shape you into a more formidable candidate. Your path to success is paved with the insights and connections you gather along the way.

Also remember, that attending interviews even when you have a job, is a way to test your profile against the market, understand if you acquire the most relevant and competitive skills and if there's any areas you may want to develop or grow in order to remain competitive in your field. You may want to keep this practice in mind.

Decoding the Interview Outcome

Unravelling the Secrets to Success

Ah, the mysterious interview outcome. It's a result of various factors that go beyond your skills and background. As someone who has played both the interviewer and interviewee roles, let me assure you that there's a whole list of elements that shape the final decision. Allow me to shed light on these factors and reveal what truly influences who gets offered the job.

Competition - A Battle of the Best and a Matter of Luck

Picture this: a fierce battleground where talented candidates clash for the same role. When there's a plethora of highly skilled applicants vying for the position, you can bet that the competition is intense. Your skills and experience alone won't guarantee success; you must find ways to stand out amidst the crowd. In these cases, a winning personality, good interview performance and a long-lasting impression would be the key to success.

Conversely, if you find yourself in a pool of less candidates, your chances of shining brightly increase. Lady Luck may smile upon you, offering a better opportunity to impress and secure that coveted job offer.

This is to suggest, you should go for any role that inspires you and you would love to see yourself doing. If you feel you don't tick all the boxes it doesn't matter, still go for it. There's plenty other unknown to you factors that can determine the final outcome. Remember, competition and chance both play their part, and you never truly know the landscape of your fellow interviewees. Give it your absolute best shot and let your brilliance shine through!

In my career and as a mentor I have come across occasions, where candidates checked all the boxes but still heard that someone else was a better fit for the role. Usually these are areas, or roles with a high demand, and it's difficult to shine through as the final decision will be made based on minor details and you can't always predict what the interviewer thinks or expects.

In the contrary, I have seen people over the moon for over-exceeding their own expectations and landing positions, they didn't believe they would be offered. This could be due to several reasons, competition, luck, chemistry with the interviewer, demand etc. If you don't bring all skills or relevant experience, but demonstrate a character ready to overcome challenges, are ready to bridge any gaps, come up to speed and deliver; these are signals that would make an interviewer or hiring manager confident that you could make a successful hire.

I have experienced this myself, with an internal role in a company I worked for, and I am forever grateful, not only to my boss who offered me this opportunity, but also to my mentor at the time who helped me overcome my silly concerns and go for what I wanted. I wanted that role, but I was overly worried, what would others think. I was fairly new to the team; my colleagues had more experience and length of service in the team and the company. I decided to go for it, thinking 'what's the worst that can happen?' Maybe they don't give me the role, but they know I am ambitious, and they will have better visibility of my skills. So I did, I applied, and I got an interview. And guess what, I got the role of my dreams at that point, because most of my team members didn't apply for the role. Of course, it was not only that, I also did great in convincing my boss that I was capable, determined and up for the job, but the circumstances were in my favour.

These are the inspiring occasions that I keep sharing as encouraging examples with my mentees, to always go for the roles you think you would love doing, even if you feel you many not 100% tick all the boxes. You should dare to put yourself forward, for what you aspire for.

If you feel insecure about trying, ask yourself one thing. 'What's the worst that could happen?' Think it through. If you see your dream role and want to apply for it, what stops you? If your worry is the fear of failure, or what will others think of your experience or your interview performance, remember that you will never achieve anything if you don't try. By applying you simply share your interest. If they invite you for an interview, they already like you. Making it to an interview stage for a job you desire, is a win as it will give you insights on relevant interviewing approaches on this role.

If your worry is what hiring managers will think, if you will embarrass yourself, put yourself in their shoes and consider what they would think about a candidate like you. There's nothing wrong with expressing an interest for a role. The opposite rather. It's good exposure to put your name out there and share what you aspire to do.

Compatibility - A Puzzle of Personalities and Values

It's not just about ticking the boxes of skills and qualifications. The hiring manager is looking for a candidate who not only fits the company values but also harmonizes with the existing team dynamics. Your personality becomes a vital piece of the puzzle.

During the interview, the hiring manager assesses your skills and delves into your personality traits, envisioning how well you would integrate into the team. If there's a glaring mismatch between your personality and the two factors mentioned above, it could significantly impact the outcome. Sometimes, a specific environment requires a softer touch or a stronger presence, and you are evaluated based on these multifaceted aspects.

Therefore, remember that not being selected in

this instance does not define your worth, as it could simply mean that this particular opportunity isn't the perfect fit for your unique talents and aspirations. Keep exploring, for there are countless paths that await where you can thrive and make a profound impact.

People & Technical Skills - Unleashing Your Potential

Beyond your technical expertise, the interviewers are keen on uncovering your soft skills and potential. They want to see your emotional intelligence, teamwork abilities, business acumen, and adaptability to thrive in a dynamic environment. Showcasing your capacity for growth and your enthusiasm to learn and develop quickly is key.

Demonstrate these skills convincingly, persuading the interviewers that you possess the qualities they seek. Your experience is just the tip of the iceberg; they want to see the depths of your potential.

For example, if you don't know a particular tool or process, it's good for you to be able to articulate during the interview, with confidence the amount of experience you have, but follow through by expressing your eagerness to learn and in what ways.

Interview Performance - Mastering the Art of Impression

Your performance during the interview speaks

volumes. It's not just about your answers; it's about the overall impression you leave behind. Arriving presentable and punctual, answering questions with finesse, being prepared, and concluding with thoughtful questions to the interviewers, all contribute to making a positive first impression. When the conversation flows freely and effortlessly, not like a dull interrogation, you know you've made a good connection. Be real, be you, and watch that bond ignite. Own your interviews like a boss!

As you can see, skills and experience are only a part of the equation. The interview outcome is a culmination of various factors coming together. It's important to note that not every candidate will excel in all areas mentioned above. The interviewer is looking for someone who meets most, if not all, of these elements—especially the ones they prioritize based on the role and their personal judgment.

Remember, an interview outcome can sometimes be subjective. Not receiving a job offer doesn't mean you lack skills in all the areas described. It simply means that you may not have hit the mark in all or most of these elements. Embrace this realization, move forward with confidence, and let your brilliance shine in your next interview.

Interview Preparation

Unlock Your Potential and Ace the Interview

Welcome to the exciting journey of interview preparation, where you have the power to unleash your full potential and conquer any interview challenge that comes your way. Prepare yourself for success by mastering the art of interview readiness and exceeding all expectations with your remarkable skills and preparedness.

Understanding the Key Elements

1. Allocate Sufficient Time

Time is an asset and investing wisely in interview preparation is crucial. By dedicating sufficient time to prepare, not only will you excel in your scheduled interview, but you will also lay a solid foundation for future interviews. Think of it as an investment that will pay off exponentially. Once you have gone through the process of preparing your responses, future interview preparations will become quicker and easier. Remember, many roles in the industry require similar skills, but tailoring your preparation to the specific job description is vital.

2. Embrace Preparation

Going into an interview unprepared is like venturing into uncharted territory without a map.

It can at times lead to discomfort, stress, and even a negative experience. Don't let that happen to you. Embrace the opportunity to prepare thoroughly, as it will enable you to showcase your true skillset effectively.

3. Harness the opportunity

When you are invited to an interview, someone is devoting their valuable time to meet and learn about you. It's an incredible opportunity that you must seize with both hands. By devoting ample time to prepare, you position yourself for success and increase your comfort level during the interview. This advantage will undoubtedly work in your favour.

4. Tailor Your Preparation

Depending on the nature of the interview, the amount of time required for preparation may vary. Some interviews may be as short as 30-60 minutes, while others can extend to 3 hours or more. The length of preparation is determined by the interview's nature and the hiring process stage.

Here's a table that reflects some of the most common interview types you may come across, with their expected duration and suggested sufficient time for you to allocate for your preparation.

Interview Type	Typical Duration	Suggested Preparation Time
Telephone Interview (Screening)	15-30 min	1-2 hours
Competency Based/ Behavioural Interview (faces to face or online)	45-60 min	4-6 hours
Automated online Interview (e.g HireVue)	30-60 min	3-5 hours
Case Study Interview	45-90 min	6-8 hours
Assessment Centre	1-2 days	8-12 hours
Technical or Skills Based Interview	45-90 min	4-6 hours
Group Interview	60-120 min	4-6 hours

5. Review the Job Description

Carefully read the job description (JD) for the role you're applying to. Highlight the skills and competencies required and think of examples from your own experiences that demonstrate each one of the skills listed. Use the S-T-A-R technique (Situation, Task, Action, Result) to structure your responses. It's normal not to have experience in every single requirement listed, so focus on emphasizing your relevant skills and willingness to learn.

Let's jump into a bit more detail, on what each

interview type entails.

Telephone Interview-Screening with a Recruiter

This interview, though not always conducted, typically involves a brief conversation with an internal or external recruiter. It serves as a shortlisting chat via phone. During this interview, the recruiter aims to provide more details about the role and assess basic high-level factors, such as your willingness to work at the office and your relevant skills.

Be prepared to answer questions related to:

- Your background, skills, and experience
- Reasons for leaving your current role
- Employment gaps
- Right to work in the country
- How your background aligns with the discussed role
- Awareness of the company and interest in the role/sector
- Flexibility to work from the office or remotely
- Salary expectations

If asked about your current salary and you prefer not to disclose it, you can be a bit more strategic and a bit vague. Refer to the Appendix on how to best answer this question.

Remember, you have the right to redirect the

question back to the interviewer, by asking them to provide the budget or salary range for this role. In this way you can possibly refrain from sharing your salary details, as they are personal and may not reflect your expectations or worth accurately. You don't want to ask less for a job that can pay you more. But at the same time, you don't want to miss a good opportunity if you ask for a salary way above the possible salary range, they can offer.

Remember, someone's current salary should not define their worth or next salary. Employees usually get a significant salary increase when they start a new job by moving to a new company. On the contrary, internal company job changes or promotions are not usually accompanied by significant salary increases, which means that someone who joined a company in an early career role i.e Associate and has since moved to different roles and had several promotions and great experience may have only seen 10% salary increase for every job change, and sometimes even lower.

To prepare effectively for this interview, make sure you familiarize yourself with the company's values, mission, CEO, and top competitors. Although you may not be directly asked about these details, incorporating relevant information into your responses can add value. Additionally, check for any recent news or articles about the company on LinkedIn, Google News and Twitter to demonstrate your informed perspective.

Furthermore, this interview serves as an early opportunity for you to gather information about the company's structure, culture (e.g., development and training opportunities, salary range, team structure), the hiring manager, the interview process stages, and how the role became available.

Competency-Based/ Behavioural Interview

Competency-based interviews and Behavioural interviews are similar in many ways, as they both aim to understand a candidate's past behaviour and performance to predict future success in a role. However, there are some subtle differences between the two.

Competency-Based Interview

These interviews specifically target the key competencies required for the role, such as teamwork, leadership, problem-solving, etc.

The questions asked, are designed around specific competencies, and candidates are asked to provide evidence of these competencies from their past experiences. The scope is more narrowly focused on the core competencies defined for the specific position. Competency based interviews aim to evaluate whether a candidate possesses the specific skills and abilities required for the job.

Example Question: "Give an example of a time when you demonstrated leadership within a team."

Behavioural Interview

Behavioural interviews concentrate on how a candidate has behaved in specific past situations, often using open-ended questions. The interviews typically begin with questions with phrases like "Tell me about a time when..." or "Describe a situation where..." Behavioural interviews may cover a broader range of topics, not always tied to specific competencies defined for the role.

The interviewer is seeking to understand how a candidate's past behaviours align with the company's culture, values, and general job requirements.

Example Question: "Tell me about a time when you had to handle a difficult team member."

In practice, these two types of interviews can overlap, and the terms are sometimes used interchangeably. Both approaches value the use of the STAR method (Situation, Task, Action, Result) to structure answers, providing clear and concise examples from the candidate's past experiences. By understanding the key competencies or behaviours sought by the interviewer, a candidate can prepare effectively for either type of interview.

Your task as the interviewee is to showcase the required skill by providing a well-structured response using the STAR technique. When utilizing the STAR technique, it's crucial to emphasize your individual actions and contributions by using the first person, "I," rather than "we." This ensures that the interviewer clearly understands your specific involvement and impact. Remember to focus on your own actions rather than actions as part of a larger group.

Additionally, it's important to highlight positive results. Try to avoid examples with negative outcomes unless the question specifically asks for a mistake, and you can demonstrate your ability to learn from it and take appropriate action to prevent its recurrence. Sharing the measures you implemented based on that learning would be an ideal positive outcome.

During these interviews, keep the below simple tips in mind to avoid unnecessary pitfalls:

Understand the question thoroughly. Ensure that your response covers the competencies they are seeking. If you didn't understand the question, feel free to ask the interviewer to repeat it.

Gather your thoughts before sharing your answer. This will help you provide a relevant and concise response without oversharing unnecessary details or fabricating information.

It's perfectly fine to not start your answer immediately and say, something like: "That's an excellent question. Would you mind giving me a moment to think that through?" or "Could I take a brief moment to consider my response?"

If you can't come up with a strong answer in 1-2 min, don't force yourself to make things up, while you speak. You can ask the interviewer to return to this question at a later stage, by saying: "Thank you for your question. I'd like to give you the most thoughtful answer possible. Would it be alright if we come back to this question at the end of our conversation? I believe I'll be able to articulate my response more effectively after reflecting on it a bit more."

Avoid providing generic responses. It's always important to provide specific examples and your actions and outcome on these. Avoid saying, I am always promoting teamwork, or I never do mistakes.

Focus on your individual contributions and actions. Ensure you use 'I' and emphasising your input, instead of 'we'. This allows you to effectively demonstrate your unique role and value add in the example you are sharing. By using 'we' you don't allow the interviewer to understand if it was your action and initiative or someone else's. It's important in these interview questions to demonstrate your own actions.

Provide recent examples. Focus on providing fairly recent professional or personal examples in your responses, ideally within a 1–2-year timeframe, will demonstrate evolution of your skills, credibility and impact. Avoid relying heavily on examples that are 3-5 years old, unless you have a compelling and valuable example to share. Overusing outdated experiences may imply a lack of recent skills acquired in your most recent roles.

Avoid too many examples from university life. It's good to cover some competency-based questions based on your educational set up with classmates i.e. teamwork, communication, time management, but ensure you also give examples from your professional experience, wherever that may have been. Too many examples from university could potentially lead the interviewer to form a perception of lack of experience and lack of professional context.

Case Study

In certain job interviews, especially for internships, graduate roles, occasionally some managerial positions and more senior roles, you may encounter a case study as part of the interview process.

The interviewer will let you know beforehand if you're to expect one, so don't worry it shouldn't be a surprise.

There are two ways candidates could be assessed for a case study, each one requires a different preparation set up.

On-the-spot Case Study During The Interview

If you're starting out in your career, such as an internship, graduate, or entry-level role, expect the case study to be a part of your assessment day.

In this setup, you don't need to worry about preparing in advance. On the day of the interview or assessment, you'll be handed a case study to read, along with some questions to ponder on. You'll typically get about 20-30 minutes for this before the interviewers return to hear your findings.

These spontaneous case studies evaluate your prioritization skills, planning abilities, conflict management, customer service acumen, innovative thinking and teamwork skills, depending on whether you're working individually or with other candidates.

When you dive into the case study, keep the company values at the forefront of your mind. If the company is known for its fast-paced, innovative culture, sharpen your focus, and brainstorm creative ideas. But if the company prizes a relaxed or inclusive atmosphere, prioritize your communication skills and cultivate an empathetic approach to others in the case study. Remember, you're not only being judged on your ideas but also on your people skills and overall approach. Be polite, considerate, and remember to showcase the skills highlighted in the job description.

In certain assessment situations, companies may opt for group case studies instead of individual ones. Here, you'd be working alongside other candidates, to analyse a specific case. After discussing it within the group, you'll need to collaboratively reach a conclusion, which you'll then present to the interviewers.

When participating in a group case study, it's not only about reaching the solution, but it's also a test of your ability to work effectively with others, influence them but also ensure you listen to them and let them speak. Problem-solving skills, and interpersonal aptitude are also part of the game.

Here are a few pointers to help you prepare:

1. Clear Understanding of Goals. Kick things off by getting to know the case study well. Understand its objectives and what's expected from the group. Pay attention to any specific roles or tasks assigned to each participant.

2. Practice Active Listening. During the group discussion, tune in to what your teammates are saying. Comprehend their viewpoints, encourage an atmosphere of open conversation and collaboration, and always respect differing opinions. If you don't agree with their point of view, don't push them in a corner, instead say that's a good point, but what about.... I feel this could also help with....."

3. Make Your Contribution Count. Take an active role in the group's decision-making process. Voice your thoughts and suggestions based on your understanding of the case study, and back them up with

logical reasoning.

4. Keep an Eye on the Clock and Stay Organized Be mindful of the time you've been given. Ensure that the group maintains focus and follows the set plan. Facilitate efficient task distribution to optimize the use of time available.

5. Showcase Professionalism and Team Spirit. Treat your team members with respect and professionalism throughout the process. Be supportive, willing to cooperate, flexible to changes, and demonstrate your capacity to be a valuable team player.

Case Study Examples

Below you will find 16 examples of case studies companies use on assessment days along with their description, and the qualities you may want to demonstrate in each case.

1. Lost at Sea or the Desert
Team members must prioritize a list of salvaged items to survive after being shipwrecked or lost in the dessert after a plane crash.
Focus: Decision making, collaboration, prioritization.

2. The Egg Drop Challenge
Teams are given various materials and must design a contraption to protect an egg from breaking when dropped from a certain height.
Focus: Creativity, problem-solving, engineering

3. Market Entry Strategy

Groups may be asked to develop a strategy for entering a new market with a specific product, considering competition, regulations, consumer behaviour, etc.

Focus: Strategic thinking, market analysis, planning

4. Corporate Social Responsibility (CSR) Plan

Participants could be tasked with creating a CSR plan that aligns with the company's goals and values.

Focus: Ethical understanding, alignment with company values

5. Project Management Simulation

Teams manage a simulated project, making decisions about budgeting, scheduling, risk management, etc., and facing challenges that require problem-solving and adaptability.

Focus: Project management, scheduling

6. Mergers and Acquisitions Scenario

Participants analyse the benefits and drawbacks of a hypothetical merger or acquisition between companies, considering financial, strategic, and cultural factors.

Focus: Financial acumen, strategic thinking, analysis

7. Crisis Management Exercise

Teams are given a hypothetical crisis situation (e.g., a PR scandal, product recall) and must develop a plan to manage and resolve the issue.

Focus: Crisis management, communication, problem solving

8. Building Challenges
Tasks like building a bridge or tower using limited materials (e.g., spaghetti and marshmallows) to test creativity, collaboration, and problem-solving.
Focus: Engineering skills, creativity, teamwork

9. Environmental Sustainability Challenge
Designing a product or service that meets specific sustainability goals, considering various environmental and economic factors.
Focus: Sustainability, innovative thinking

10. Ethical Dilemma Scenarios
Groups must navigate complex ethical situations relevant to the business world, requiring thoughtful analysis and decision-making.
Focus: Ethical reasoning, analysis, decision-making

11. Negotiation Exercise
Teams may be asked to negotiate a complex business deal or resolve a conflict between parties, assessing negotiation and mediation skills.
Focus: Negotiation skills, conflict resolution, diplomacy

12. Product Development Exercise
Participants could be tasked with creating a new product concept, considering design, marketing, production, and other aspects.
Focus: Creativity, product design, marketing

13. Virtual Team Challenge
Remote or virtual team exercises may simulate the challenges and opportunities of collaborating across different time zones and cultures.
Focus: Remote collaboration, cross-cultural communication

14. Disaster Recovery Planning
Creating a plan to ensure business continuity in the event of a natural disaster, cyber-attack, or other catastrophic events.
Focus: Planning, risk assessment, IT

15. Customer Service Scenario
Teams must develop a strategy to improve customer service, handling various challenges and feedback.
Focus: Customer service skills, empathy, problem-solving

16. Health and Safety Compliance Exercise
Designing a workplace health and safety program that complies with regulations and best practices.
Focus: Compliance understanding, safety awareness, planning

These exercises provide insights into candidates' abilities to think critically, work collaboratively, communicate effectively, and apply knowledge in a practical context. The above examples are just insights from case studies used from different companies and experienced by different candidates in different periods of time. You can use them as an idea, of what you can expect when preparing for an assessment centre. Different companies and industries may have specific scenarios tailored to their particular needs and values.

Case Study Preparation Ahead of the Interview

For roles requiring more experience, you might be given a case study to prepare in advance and present during your interview.

This preparation requires careful time management. You'll need to thoroughly analyse th e case, gather your insights, and plan how best to present your findings. Creating a few slides might be a good approach but remember to keep your presentation time in mind.

Case studies aren't just about the analysis; they're about presentation too. Your preparation time should include not just research and slide preparation, but also rehearsing your presentation. Your communication, presentation skills, ability to influence, and time management are all under the microscope alongside the case study content. So, rehearse well, be clear and concise, engage your audience, and always reserve about 5-10 minutes for questions.

Typically, preparing a case study for an interview could take between 6-8 hours, depending on the complexity of the case and the role's level. For instance, you might be given an Excel file to analyse and asked to present your findings through a few slides. This task will test your analytical skills as you identify key data points and any less obvious insights.

When it comes to your presentation, remember that content is as important as aesthetics. A clean, attractive slide deck is essential, but so is your verbal delivery of the findings. Presentation skills are crucial, so balance your time equally between slide creation and presentation rehearsal.

A handy tip for mastering case study presentations is to rehearse aloud, ensuring you stay within your allotted time. If you're given 30 minutes, aim to finish within 25 minutes, leaving enough room for questions. A brilliant presentation is a blend of comprehensive analysis, clear communication, and impeccable timing.

Individual case studies that require preparation and presentation are common for entry-level roles, especially in fields like consulting, marketing, finance, and analytics. For a comprehensive list of case studies, tasks, and roles that candidates may encounter, please refer to the table below, where you can find examples.

These examples are designed to illustrate the variety of scenarios you could encounter based on the roles you are interviewing for. They are meant to provide a meaning flavour of what to expect, they are not exhaustive, nor guaranteed to be part of every interview.

Case Study	Task	Roles
Competitor Analysis	Analysing competitor products, identifying strengths and weaknesses, recommending strategies.	Marketing Analyst, Product Manager
New Market Evaluation	Evaluating potential of entering a new market, considering demand, competition, regulations.	Business Analyst, Market Research Analyst
Supply Chain Optimisation	Analysing supply chain data to identify inefficiencies, proposing improvements.	Operations Analyst, Supply Chain Coordinator

Customer Satisfaction Analysis	Reviewing customer feedback, identifying trends, recommending strategies.	Customer Success Manager, Sales Analyst
Product Launch Proposal	Creating a proposal for launching a new product, including market analysis, strategy, pricing.	Product Manager, Marketing Associate
Investment Evaluation	Analysing ROI for a project or acquisition, considering risks, costs, growth.	Financial Analyst, Investment Banking Analyst
Social Media Performance Review	Analysing social media performance, identifying successful content, proposing strategy.	Social Media Coordinator, Digital Marketing Analyst
Cost Reduction Strategy	Identifying areas to reduce costs without compromising quality, proposing a plan.	Operations Analyst, Compliance Office
Employee Engagement Plan	Reviewing employee satisfaction data, proposing a plan to increase engagement, retention.	HR Analyst, Talent Acquisition Specialist
Risk Assessment	Evaluating risks associated with a business decision or project, recommending strategies.	Risk Analyst, Compliance Officer
Sales Forecasting	Using historical sales data to forecast	Sales Analyst, Business

	future sales, recommending strategies.	Development Associate
Website Performance Analysis	Analysing website traffic, user behaviour, conversion rates, recommending improvements.	SEO Specialist, Web Analyst

Assessment Centre

Commonly used for graduate schemes or internships, assessment centres assess candidates through various activities. These may include individual competency-based interviews, case studies, and group work exercises, as well as a tour around the office promises, shopfloors, or labs (depending on the company). Assessment centres usually run for a fully day 4-6 hours.

Preparing for the assessment centre understand the objective of each assessment parts, actively listen, contribute meaningfully, manage time effectively, and always demonstrate professionalism and teamwork during the day. This includes breaks, lunches and time spent in the offices, even outside of the interview sessions. You should of course be relaxed, when having a break, but remember you want to always make a good impression. Have questions in mind you may want to ask anyone accompanying you, around their experience, the company culture etc.

Here's what you might expect, along with some

tips on how to prepare.

Components of an Assessment Centre

Group Exercises: Working with others to solve problems, make decisions, or undertake tasks. It assesses teamwork, communication, and leadership.

Individual Exercises: Such as case studies, presentations, or written tests to evaluate skills like analysis, creativity, and technical expertise.

Interviews: Including competency-based or behavioural interviews to assess your motivations, values, and fit for the role and company.

Psychometric Tests: Assessing personality traits, cognitive abilities, or specific skills, such as numerical reasoning.

Role-Playing: Simulating real job scenarios to assess how you handle specific tasks, challenges, or interactions.

In-Tray Exercises: Managing a simulated workload, prioritizing tasks, and making decisions as if you were in the role.

Preparing for an Assessment Centre

1. Understand the Role and Competencies: Research the job description, required skills, and competencies. Understand what the company is looking for in an ideal candidate.

2. Practice Typical Exercises: If you know what kinds of exercises will be used, practice them. This might include group activities, case studies, or psychometric tests.

3. Prepare for Interviews: Understand common interview questions, especially those that are competency-based, and prepare your answers using the STAR (Situation, Task, Action, Result) method.

4. Develop Presentation Skills: If presentations are required, practice delivering concise and engaging talks. Consider joining a local Toastmasters club or practicing with friends.

5. Work on Teamwork and Leadership: Engage in group activities where you can practice working with others, taking the lead when necessary, and contributing positively to a team dynamic.

6. Review Basic Numeracy and Literacy Skills: If aptitude tests are part of the assessment, review basic mathematics, data interpretation, and verbal reasoning skills.

7. Research the Company: Understand the company's culture, values, products, and industry to demonstrate your genuine interest and alignment with their mission.

8. Ask for Information: Don't hesitate to ask the company for any details about the assessment centre, such as the schedule,

what to expect, and what to bring with you.

9. Take Care of Yourself: Get a good night's sleep before the assessment, eat well, and dress appropriately. Bring any necessary materials, such as identification, pens, or a notepad.

10. Keep in mind that an assessment centre is not only an opportunity for the company to evaluate you but also a chance for you to understand more about the company, the role, and whether it's a good fit for you. Engage with the process, ask questions, and treat it as a learning experience.

Companies continue to run assessments after the COVID-19 pandemic. The nature and format of these assessments might have changed to accommodate safety guidelines and the shift to remote work, but the underlying purpose remains the same.

In-Person Assessment

Some companies have returned to in-person assessment centres, particularly in regions where COVID-19 restrictions have eased. They may implement safety measures such as social distancing, mask requirements, sanitization protocols, and reduced group sizes to ensure the safety of both candidates and assessors.

Virtual Assessments

Many companies have also adapted their

assessment processes to virtual formats. Virtual assessment centres utilize video conferencing tools, online testing platforms, and collaborative software to conduct exercises, interviews, and tests. Virtual assessments allow companies to continue evaluating candidates without physical contact, catering to remote work environments and global candidate pools.

Hybrid Models

Some organizations may use a combination of in-person and virtual assessments, depending on the role, location, and specific needs of the assessment process. A hybrid approach might involve online testing and virtual interviews, followed by an in-person group exercise or final interview.

Preparing for Virtual Assessments

If you're participating in a virtual assessment centre, here are some additional tips to prepare:

- Test Your Technology. Ensure your Internet connection, camera, microphone, and any required software are working well in advance. If you need to use a new application for the first time, like Zoom or Microsoft Team, ensure you have installed the app, and it runs properly in your device. Avoid unnecessary delays on the day, due to set up or technical difficulties.

- Create a Professional Environment. Choose a quiet, well-lit space for your virtual assessment, free from distractions.

- Prepare as you would for an In-Person Assessment Dress professionally, have necessary materials ready, and review the schedule and expectations for the day.

- Practice Virtual Collaboration. If group exercises are part of the assessment, practice working with others online, using tools like shared documents or virtual whiteboards.

Regardless of the format, the fundamental principles of preparation remain the same. Research the company, understand the role and competencies being assessed, practice relevant exercises, and approach the assessment with a positive and engaged attitude. Whether in-person or virtual, companies are still invested in finding the right candidates, and assessment centres remain a valuable tool in that process.

Online Interview

In the digital era, online interviews have become increasingly popular. Whether it's through HireVue, Microsoft Teams, or Zoom, the following tips will help you make a positive impression.

Technical Setup: Ensure you have stable internet connection, a working webcam, and a distraction-free environment. Test your equipment beforehand, make sure your microphone and sound are working fine. Do a test if needed, by using your camera/video app and recording yourself. Then play it back and ensure you are heard.

Dress Professionally: Dress the part, just as you would for an in-person interview. It boosts confidence and demonstrates your seriousness.

Avoid disruptions: phone, flatmates or family members jumping in or making noise. Make sure you have arranged to take the assessment centre or any interviews in a quiet, personal space.

Body Language and Eye Contact: Maintain good eye contact by looking directly at the camera. Sit upright, use appropriate hand gestures, and exude confidence throughout the interview.

Be natural: Avoid using your laptop screen to read out to the interviewer prepared responses or notes, as loss of eye contact and engagement is really easy to sport and does not make a good impression.

Practice, Practice, Practice: Familiarize yourself with common interview questions and practice responding to them. Conduct mock interviews with a friend or family member to gain confidence and refine your answers. You can even try to record yourself, and listen back to what you said. I am not a fun of recording myself, but it helps me to practice out loud, so I can hear myself and sense my flow.

Research and Engage: Prior to the interview, research the company thoroughly. Understand its values, mission, recent news, and key projects.

During the interview, demonstrate your knowledge and engage with the interviewer by asking thoughtful questions.

Online Research: Allocate time to conduct online research on the company. Visit their website, explore their LinkedIn page, and search for recent news articles. Look for information on the company's background, mission, purpose, values, competitors, CEO, and board. This research will help you understand the company's culture and position yourself confidently during the interview.

Master Your Elevator Pitch

An elevator pitch is a brief and persuasive speech that you can use to spark interest in what you or your organization does. It's called an "elevator pitch" because it should be concise enough to present during a brief elevator ride, typically around 30 seconds to 1 minute.

The goal of an elevator pitch is to provide a clear, engaging summary that piques the listener's interest and invites further conversation. It's often used by job seekers, entrepreneurs, sales professionals, or anyone looking to make a strong, quick connection with someone else.

Craft a concise and engaging elevator pitch that introduces yourself in a compelling way. Your elevator pitch should highlight who you are, what you do, and what you aspire to achieve. Practice delivering it within 30 to 60 seconds, focusing on key points that will leave a lasting impression.

Components of an Effective Elevator Pitch

- Introduction: Start by introducing yourself and your background.
- What You Do: Clearly and concisely explain what you do by focusing on the aspects that are most relevant to the listener.
- Unique Value Proposition: Highlight what sets you apart from others, such as a particular skill, product, or approach.
- Goal or Call to Action: Depending on the context, you might include a specific request, like asking for a meeting, or a more general invitation to learn more.
- Engaging and Memorable: Use language that is clear, enthusiastic, and tailored to the listener. Avoid jargon and aim to make a personal connection.

If you're a recent graduate seeking a job in marketing, your pitch might look something like this:

Hi, I'm [Your Name], a recent graduate from [University] with a degree in Marketing. During my studies, I led a project that increased student engagement with our campus app by 40%. I'm passionate about leveraging data to create targeted marketing strategies. I'm currently looking for a role where I can apply these skills to help a company grow its online presence. Could I share more details over coffee sometime?

In the fast-paced world of interviews, it's crucial to have a well-crafted elevator pitch up your sleeve. Think of it as a concise and impactful introduction that you can deliver in the time it takes to ride an elevator with someone. Your elevator pitch should encapsulate your unique story, strengths, and career aspirations, leaving a lasting impression on your listeners.

Here are a few more examples to inspire you:

"Hi, I'm Alex. As a marketing professional with a passion for storytelling, I've helped brands connect with their audience through compelling content strategies. With a keen eye for trends and a knack for building authentic relationships, I strive to create meaningful campaigns that drive results."

"Hey there, I'm Emily. As a software engineer, I thrive on solving complex problems and creating innovative solutions. I've collaborated on cutting-edge projects that have transformed user experiences and optimized systems. My goal is to continue pushing boundaries and contributing to the ever-evolving tech landscape."

"Nice to meet you! I'm Sarah, a recent graduate in finance. With a strong analytical background and a knack for data interpretation, I've assisted in financial forecasting and risk analysis for major organizations. I'm determined to leverage my skills and make a positive impact in the world of finance."

Craft your own elevator pitch by focusing on your

unique skills, experiences, and aspirations. Practice delivering it with confidence, ensuring that it flows smoothly and highlights your most impressive qualities. A well-crafted elevator pitch will make you memorable and open doors to exciting opportunities.

Identify Your Top 3 Challenges and Achievements

Having these available in a way to share with STAR technique can help you answer almost any interview question. This is because, these examples are very strong, are real and can be most likely fitting more than one answer. If you have thought through 3 of your biggest challenges and how you overcame them, as well as 3 of your biggest achievement you should be in a great place to conquer any competency based interview.

To come up with these examples, reflect on your life, educational, and professional experiences. These should be genuine examples that showcase your ability to overcome difficult situations and achieve significant milestones.

Prepare Your Questions for the interviewer(s)

Towards the end of the interview, you will likely be given the opportunity to ask questions. It's important to have a few, usually 2-3, well-thought-out questions prepared as part of your interview preparation. Remember, even during this phase, you are being assessed, so take advantage of this opportunity to make a positive impression.

Having no questions for the interviewer can be perceived as a lack of preparation or interest in the role. Therefore, take a few minutes to think about what you would like to ask the interviewers during the interview.

I strongly advise candidates to avoid common procedural questions, like "When can I expect to hear back?", "What are the next steps?" or "What are the benefits that you offer?". These are legitimate questions but can be straightforward and can easily be answered by the recruiter or hiring manager at a later stage outside the interview. Treat the opportunity to ask questions more strategically, so you can make the difference amongst other candidates and leave a long-lasting impression to the interviewers.

Check out on the Appendix, an extensive list of proposed questions that you can ask at the end of each interview.

Tips to consider when preparing your Questions

- Tailor to the Conversation. If something specific was mentioned during the interview that intrigued you, don't hesitate to ask for more information.

- Be Mindful of Time. Recognize that there

may be limited time at the end of the interview, so prioritize your most important questions.

- Avoid Overly Personal or Inappropriate Questions. Focus on the role, the company, the team, and your potential fit within the organization.

- Research Ahead of Time. Avoid asking questions that are easily answered through basic research on the company's website, like company culture. Your questions should reflect a deeper interest and understanding of the organization.

Unlocking Insights

Leveraging Online Platforms and AI for Interview Success

LinkedIn

Use LinkedIn strategically to gain insights into professionals working in similar roles at the company.

While maintaining professionalism, gather information about their background and skillset. Avoid directly approaching individuals for help with interview questions unless they have indicated willingness to assist.

If you have an interview or have reached the offer stage, there's no harm in contacting employees on LinkedIn, from this company who seem to work in the same department or team and say that you are in the interview process or have just received an offer and would appreciate if they could share their experience in terms of company culture and if they are happy there. You can do the same with people who have also worked there but left to move on in a different company. They may also be even more open to share insights. This is an indirect approach and people are usually happy to share their experiences.

For example, you can use one of the Networking templates in the Appendix, to approach someone, in order to gain insights about a company you are interviewing with. It's essential to be clear, courteous, and specific in your request.

You can also use Linked in to build your Network. Connect with alumni, industry professionals and recruiters. Engaging with your network can open doors to opportunities and provide insights to various roles and companies. Ask professors, colleagues or mentors to write recommendations highlighting your strengths and achievements.

Glassdoor

It's a popular platform that provides insights into companies through employee reviews, salary data and interview experiences. This information can help you understand what to expect in the interview and how to prepare. While not all companies may listed, this platform can provide valuable information about interview experiences and the work environment.

Utilize salary information to understand the compensation range for the role you're applying for, which can aid in negotiation if you receive an offer.

There's more free platforms you can use for similar company insights

- Indeed: Indeed provides company reviews, salary information, and job listings. It's free to use and widely recognized as a valuable resource for job seekers.

- Payscale: If you're looking specifically for salary information, Payscale is a great resource. It offers detailed compensation data for various roles across industries.

- Vault: Vault provides information on companies, including culture, interviews, and rankings across different industries. Some content might be behind a paywall, but there's valuable free information as well.

- Kununu: Similar to Glassdoor, Kununu offers employee reviews and insights into company culture, benefits, and more.

- Comparably: This platform focuses on company culture and compensation data, offering insights into what it's like to work at different organizations.

ChatGPT

If you have not yet familiarised yourself with ChatGPT, maybe it's time you jump right into it and take advantage of AI to support you with your interview preparation. Not only can it help you practice answering common interview questions, but it can also provide you with gathered insights on the business and culture of the company you're interviewing with.

You can ask ChatGPT to provide examples of questions that have been asked in previous interviews for similar roles or industries, allowing you to familiarize yourself with the types of questions you may encounter. Additionally, ChatGPT can help you brainstorm and refine your responses to ensure they align with the company's values and objectives. The more you practice the more confident you will become.

While these resources can provide valuable information, it's essential to approach them with discernment. Every interview experience is unique, and the company may have evolved since the reviews were posted. Use these insights as a supplement to your overall preparation but rely primarily on your own research and self-assessment.

By following these tips and dedicating time to each aspect of interview preparation, you'll be well-equipped to showcase your skills, experiences, and enthusiasm during the interview.

By supercharging your interview preparation using these strategies, you'll not only enhance your chances of success in the current interview but also develop valuable skills that will serve you well throughout your career. Remember to practice, refine your responses, and approach each interview with confidence and enthusiasm. Your dedication and preparation will set you apart from the competition and bring you closer to your desired career opportunities.

Recognize Your Personality Traits

Have you ever noticed how you shine in certain social situations? Or maybe you've caught yourself excelling when given some quiet time to think? That could be your personality at work, and it's something to celebrate.

In this section, we're not about putting labels on people or boxing them into categories. No, that's not our intention. Instead, the goal is, for any who feel they relate with some of these traits, to take a closer look, as these could be beneficial to your interview approach and preparation.

These insights aren't rules. They're simply meant to help you understand yourself better and to make those interviews feel more like you.

Advice and Tips for Introverts

Introverts excel when well-prepared. Spend time thoroughly researching the company, role, and common interview questions to boost your confidence. Practice answers to potential questions, and rather than trying to dominate the conversation, concentrate on providing thoughtful, well-considered responses. Have insightful questions ready to show genuine interest in the company and the role, and don't forget to leverage your active listening skills, a common strength among introverts. While you may sometimes overthink your answers or come across as reserved, focusing on showcasing your deep knowledge, attention to detail, problem-solving skills, and adaptability can set you apart.

Advice and Tips for Extroverts

As an extrovert, your vibrant personality can energize the interview. Leverage your energy by creating dynamic and engaging conversations, sharing stories that illustrate your skills and qualifications. Engage with the interviewer confidently, highlight your enthusiasm for the role and company, and remember to emphasize teamwork as one of your strengths. While extroverts can sometimes overshadow the interviewer or jump into questions without thinking through their responses, ensuring that you give space to the interviewer, stick to the STAR technique, and utilize your charisma positively can lead to success.

Advice and Tips for Ambiverts

Ambiverts have the unique ability to balance both introverted and extroverted tendencies. Leverage this by switching between active listening and engaging conversation as the situation requires. Adapt to the interviewer's cues, connect authentically by sharing insights and experiences, and showcase your versatility in both team settings and independent tasks. Although you might sometimes struggle to find a balance or appear indecisive, focusing on your adaptability, willingness to take initiative, and effective communication can showcase your unique strengths.

Your personality type, be it introverted, extroverted, or ambiverted, comes with unique strengths and challenges. Recognizing these and adapting them to the context of the interview can lead to a more authentic and effective presentation of yourself. Embrace your individuality, and let it shine throughout the interview process. Your unique fingerprint could be the key that sets you apart from the crowd.

The Interview Day

When you step into that interview room, you're not just showcasing your skills and qualifications, you're projecting a version of yourself that is confident, capable, and absolutely ready for the role.

The essence of who you are speaks not just through words, but through the unspoken language of voice tone and body cues. This is your moment to shine, and it's crucial to wield the magic of voice tone and body language to your advantage.

Imagine this: Your body is a canvas, and confidence is the masterpiece you paint upon it. Every gesture, every posture, it all contributes to a portrayal of the confident professional you are. A firm handshake, not too tight yet conveying strength, sets the stage for a dynamic interaction. As you engage in conversation, let your hands accompany your words—a subtle dance that underscores your points. It's not about extravagance; it's about creating a symphony of trust.

In a face-to-face encounter, a genuine smile transforms the atmosphere. It's not just a show of positivity; it's a reflection of the relaxed, authentic version of yourself, someone who's comfortable in their own skin. Even if your interview is over the phone, don't underestimate the power of a smile.

Believe it or not, your voice carries your emotions; a smile on your lips translates into warmth on the other end of the line.

Your body's language speaks volumes. Crossing arms creates an unnecessary barrier, a distance between you and your interviewers. Uncross them, and let your openness create a bridge of connection. When seated, maintain a professional posture; legs crossed, but not in a manner that suggests indifference. Sit forward, subtly leaning in to show engagement.

Those jitters can manifest in the form of leg-shaking, a nervous tick that's all too common. But remember, this is your opportunity to shine. Awareness is your ally; gently halt the leg's rhythm and let your poised presence take centre stage.

As you speak, let your voice resonate with assurance. A steady, calm voice is not just a reflection of confidence, but a testament to your excitement to be there. Embrace the opportunity you have and treat every question as a chance to showcase your capabilities.

For those with naturally soft voices, don't let that become a hurdle. Channel the fire of your determination into your voice. Speak up and let your words echo with clarity. Every answer, every interaction, should be crisp and audible. Prepare by practicing at home, allowing your responses to flow naturally. Envision the interview as a dialogue, a conversation where your voice is unwavering and your presence magnetic.

This is your journey, your canvas to paint. Every gesture, every intonation, they're all strokes that weave your narrative of capability and potential. This interview is not just an encounter; it's an opportunity to shine, to show who you are and why you're the perfect fit. Embrace the energy of possibility and exude the confidence that lies within you. Your voice, your body—unleash them as instruments of your professional prowess, and let your presence resonate with success. You're ready, and the world is ready for you.

Post Interview Self-Reflection

As your interview draws to a close and you make your way out, it's the perfect moment to pause and reflect on the experience you've just had. This introspective moment allows you to assess how the interview went and gain valuable insights into your performance.

Take a moment to consider your feelings immediately after the interview. How did you feel during the conversation? Did you answer confidently, or were there moments of uncertainty? Reflect on your overall impression of the interview's flow and atmosphere.

Consider how you answered the questions. Were your responses aligned with the qualities and skills you wanted to highlight? Were there any questions that caught you off guard? Reflect on the moments you feel particularly proud of and identify areas where you believe you could have performed better.

Keeping a record of your reflections is a valuable practice. Jot down your thoughts, emotions, and any standout moments from the interview. This serves as a personal debriefing, allowing you to revisit your experience and learn from it. Additionally, if you have multiple interviews in progress, these notes can help you differentiate.

Below, you can find a comprehensive interview tracking template that can help you to capture the nuances of each interview. By documenting not only the questions asked, but also your emotions, feedback, and post-interview actions, you gain a deeper understanding of your journey, enabling you to make more informed decisions.

Let's delve into the structure and benefits of an interview tracker. Here's a list of items you could track on an interview tracking template.

Aspect	Details
Interview Date	Date of the interview
Company	Name of the company you interviewed with
Position	Job title, role you interviewed for
Interview Type	Indicate if it was phone scree. Technical, behavioural etc
Interviewers	Names and roles of interviewers
Questions Asked	List key interview questions and your responses
Emotions	How did you feel before, during and after the interview. Use a scale (1 to 5) or keywords
Cultures and Environment	Describe the company's workplace culture and your impression of the environment.
Interview Process	Detail the stages, duration and format of the interview process
Feedback and Offer	Note any feedback or comments you received from the interviewers. If an offer was extended, record the details.
Salary Discussion	Document any salary or compensation discussions

Tracking your interviews offers a range of benefits, including the ability to engage in self-reflection, identifying patterns in question types, strengths, and areas for improvement. It facilitates data-driven decision-making, aiding you in making informed choices regarding job opportunities that align with your goals.

Additionally, it promotes continuous personal growth, allowing you to monitor your evolving emotions and insights as you progress through interviews. You can also use tracking to monitor post-interview actions such as sending thank you emails and evaluating their impact. Ultimately, interview tracking supports your personal development by fostering a growth mindset through active learning from each interview experience.

While the tracking template can be created in tools like Microsoft Excel or Google Sheets, consider using digital note-taking apps, dedicated interview tracking apps, or specialized job search platforms for enhanced organization and accessibility."

There are several online tools and apps available that can help individuals track their interview experiences and job search progress. Here are a few options:

- Huntr: A comprehensive job search organizer that lets you track job applications, interviews, and follow-ups. It also offers integration with popular job boards and Chrome extension.

- Notion: A versatile note-taking and organization tool. You can create customized databases to track interview details, companies, and notes.

- Trello: A visual project management tool. Create boards for each job application or interview, add cards for details, and move them through different stages.

- JibberJobber: Offers tools for job seekers to track job applications, networking contacts, and interview details.

- JobScan: While primarily a tool to optimize your resume for applicant tracking systems (ATS), it also provides interview tracking features.

- Excel/Google Sheets: You can always create your own tracking system using spreadsheet software, customizing columns and categories to suit your needs.

I highly recommend you try these out and select a tool or app that aligns with your preferences, needs, and the level of detail you want to track. Some of these tools may offer free versions or trials, so you can explore and see which one works best for you.

The Power of the 'Thank You' Note

Once you've taken time to reflect, consider sending a simple thank you email to your interviewers. Express your gratitude for their time and the opportunity to learn more about the company and the role. A gracious thank you demonstrates professionalism and courtesy. Even if you feel, you may not have done as well as you may have wanted, still follow up and show your professionalism.

When composing your thank you email, keep it focused on appreciation and respect. Avoid reiterating your skills or qualifications, as you've already showcased them during the interview. The goal is to leave a positive impression without overwhelming the interviewers with additional information.

While a thank you email is not obligatory, sending one out of courtesy can further highlight your professionalism and enthusiasm. If you have the email addresses of the interviewers (which you can often find in the interview invitation), consider sending your note on the same day or within 24 to 48 hours.

In the era of virtual interviews, gathering email addresses is often easier, and expressing gratitude becomes more convenient. Your 'thank you' note serves as a small, but meaningful connection in a digital age.

For further insights on the importance of interview tracking and additional strategies for navigating the interview process, refer to the comprehensive information available in the appendix.

Remember, reflecting on your interviews and expressing gratitude through thank you notes are steps that contribute to your overall professional presence and can set you on a path to success in your job search journey.

Waiting to Hear Back

Waiting to hear back after an interview can be a nerve-wracking experience, especially if you are not entirely sure about the timelines, of when they are getting back to you.

Here's some advice, to help you navigate this time.

If the interviewers specified a specific date when they would contact you by, give them a day or two of leeway before considering any follow-up.

Now, if the specified date has passed and you haven't received any communication, it's completely appropriate to follow up. This shows your continued interest in the role and initiative.

In the scenario, that you were not informed about when you should expect to hear back, I would suggest you wait for about 2 weeks from your interview date, as this should be a reasonable timeframe.

When following up, ensure you keep your tone polite and professional. You can express your continued interest in the position and inquire about the status of your application. Sending an email is the preferred method of follow-up. It's less intrusive and gives the recipient the time to respond at their convenience.

I totally appreciate, that waiting until you hear can trigger anxiety, but there are many coping mechanisms that can ease your mind, in the interim.

For example, you can make a decision, on a follow-up date and set a reminder. This should prevent you from constantly checking your phone and email for updates.

In the meanwhile, try to engage in hobbies, exercise, or spend time with loved ones to keep your mind off the waiting.

You should also continue applying and interviewing with other companies. This can help ease the pressure of waiting for a single response.

Keep in mind that the hiring process takes time, and delays can occur due to various reasons. It's not necessarily a reflection of your performance. When it's time to follow up, do so respectfully. Avoid aggressive or pushy language. Express your continued interest and respect for their timeline.

Below I am sharing an example template, of a polite follow-up email when you haven't heard back from the company after the expected timeline.

Subject: Follow-Up Regarding [Position] Interview

Dear [Interviewer's Name or Hiring Manager's Name],

I hope this email finds you well. I wanted to express my continued interest in the [Position] role and inquire about the status of my application. I had the pleasure of interviewing for the position on [Interview Date], and I'm eagerly looking forward to the opportunity to potentially join the [Company] team.

I understand that timelines can sometimes shift, and I genuinely appreciate your efforts in the hiring process. If there are any updates or additional information you need from my end, please don't hesitate to let me know.

Thank you for your time and consideration. I look forward to hearing from you whenever it's convenient.

Best regards,

[Your Name]

[Your Phone Number]

The goal is to express your interest while being respectful of their time and process.

Managing Interview Outcome

Receiving a job offer

Take a moment to celebrate this achievement! YOU made it! Receiving an offer is a testament to your skills and qualifications.

After having a big scream, jump or whatever expresses yourself better, you should take a moment to yourself, and not rush into accepting the offer instantly without having a chance to review the details.

Of course, you should express your gratitude and excitement, to whoever is communicating the great news to you, and let them know you like to have the opportunity to review the offer details. If you have not received the details, ask if they can send you the offer details in writing via email.

When you receive a formal offer letter, via email including a benefits package, the salary details and proposed start date, you need to consider a few things before you say accept the offer.

Ensure that you review the offered salary, benefits package (healthcare, retirement plans, etc.), and any bonuses. Ensure the job title, responsibilities, and expectations align with your career goals. Confirm the workplace location and any commuting requirements. Understand the expected work hours and any flexibility required, if any.

Consider your career goals. Does the position align with your short-term and long-term career aspirations? Then proceed with assessing if the company's values and culture resonate with you. Consider how the job aligns with your personal values and work-life balance.

Then you can negotiate if required. If for example, the salary offered is not in line with your expectations, consider negotiating for a higher salary based on research and market rates. If certain benefits are missing or feel inadequate, discuss the possibility of improvements.

If you have questions or concerns, reach out to them, to clarify before deciding.

Pay attention to timing. If the employer sets a deadline for your response, ensure you have enough time to evaluate the offer, and you respond within the timelines to ensure you don't miss the offer. If timing is not provided, ensure you ask what the timelines for you are to accept. You should have approximately 5 days max to make a decision.

This is critical, if you accept an offer after a few days, it may no longer be available to you. Ensure you are clear in your engagements with the recruiter. I can share with you from first hand, as I lost an offer for a graduate scheme from a huge leading tech company, due to miscommunication with the recruiter. I had even received a contract and while I was negotiating my location and waiting for another contract to be issued, my initial offer was given to someone else within a matter of days. I could not believe it, but indeed there was no offer for me at the end. Awful experience, not ideal planning from the organisation's side, but it can happen. Lesson learnt here, when receiving an offer, thank them, express your enthusiasm and even if you want time to consider the offer, ask for clear timelines on the response time, or indicate you will need time to consider the offer and will return within 24-48 hours. Being professional and respectful, you should try to respond within a matter of a couple of days, no later than 3-4 days.

Regardless of your decision you should express gratitude for the offer and the time they invested in you. If you decide to accept the offer, respond promptly, confirming your acceptance and any next steps. If you decide not to accept, respond professionally and courteously, thanking them for the opportunity.

Keep in mind, that accepting a job offer is a significant commitment. Take the time you need to weigh your options, align the offer with your career goals, and ensure it's the right fit for you.

Handling an offer when expecting another one

When you receive an offer but are waiting to hear back from another interview, it's important to handle the situation thoughtfully. Here's a suggested approach to manage this without risking losing the current offer:

Respond to the offer promptly, expressing gratitude for the opportunity and their interest in your candidacy.

Politely explain that you're excited about the offer but would like some time to carefully consider it. This is a common request and most employers understand that candidates need time to make an informed decision.

Ask if there's a specific deadline by which they would need your decision. This will give you a clear idea of how much time you have to make your decision.

Let them know that you're diligently evaluating your options to make the best decision for your career, and that you'll get back to them within the specified timeframe.

If possible, reach out to the company where you're waiting for a response. Politely inquire about the status of your application and if there's any indication of when you might hear back.

Use this time to thoroughly evaluate the current offer, comparing it with your expectations and the potential opportunity you're waiting for.

If you're interested in the current offer but have certain concerns (salary, benefits, etc.), consider negotiating those points during this process.

Within the given timeframe, make a decision

based on the information you have. If the other interview doesn't provide a response within that time, you'll need to decide whether to accept the current offer or decline it.

Once you've made your decision, communicate it promptly and professionally to the company that extended the offer. If you accept, express your enthusiasm for the role. If you decline, thank them for the opportunity.

Remember that it's acceptable to ask for more time to make an informed decision. Most employers understand that candidates may be in the midst of other interview processes. Just ensure you communicate transparently and professionally throughout the process.

No offer

Not receiving a job offer can be quite disheartening, and I want you to know that your feelings of disappointment are valid. But in this moment, allow yourself to express your immediate emotions. But then, I encourage you to take a step back and recognize that there's still a reason to celebrate.

You came so close. Though you might not have an offer in hand right now, remember that the decision-making process involves numerous factors. The interview experience you recently had is a powerful asset that you now carry, and has the potential to fuel your future interviews with a newfound confidence.

Even though you may not be moving forward with this particular opportunity, the experience isn't in vain. It might lead to feedback on your performance, which is a valuable chance for growth. There's also the potential for gaining insights into the industry and forming connections within the company.

Should you receive feedback from the company on your interview performance, embrace it wholeheartedly. Constructive feedback is like a compass guiding you towards improvement for future interviews. It's important to remember that a rejection doesn't define your worth or skills. The process is complex, influenced by fit, timing, and a variety of internal factors.

This moment is a chance to nurture growth. Reflect on areas where your interview skills could flourish. Whether it's refining your responses, practicing particular questions, or polishing your overall communication, this experience is a catalyst for positive change.

As you continue, remember to maintain your professionalism. Respond to the rejection with a heartfelt note expressing gratitude for the opportunity to interview and your enduring interest in their company. Your professionalism, even in the face of disappointment, can create a lasting impression for potential future opportunities.

One setback is not a defining chapter in your journey. Maintain a positive outlook and keep applying for other positions. The lessons you've gathered from this experience can be woven into the fabric of your future interviews, guiding you towards better outcomes.

While it's natural to wonder about what could have been, I encourage you not to linger too long on the feelings of rejection. Instead, focus on moving forward. The world of opportunities is vast, and this rejection doesn't diminish your potential to find the perfect fit elsewhere.

Continue nurturing your professional network. Remember that connections have the potential to lead to unexpected opportunities. The job search journey involves its share of ups and downs, and your resilience will be your greatest ally.

Reflect upon your interview experience and consider how you might reshape or adjust your approach for future interviews. Growth comes from these moments of introspection and refinement.

Every interview is a stepping stone along your path. Even rejections contribute to your personal and professional development. Stay determined, keep honing your skills, and remain open to the multitude of opportunities that await you. Your journey is marked by growth and possibilities.

A Parting Note on Owning Your Interview Journey

You've made it to the end of this guide, but really, this is just the beginning of something incredible. Interviews aren't old-fashioned hurdles to leap over; they're your virtual stages, where you get to strut your stuff, connect with like-minded professionals, and explore worlds you've never seen before.

Didn't get the job? No sweat. That's not a fail; it's a level-up. Every interview, every handshake or Zoom call, is an experience in your personal growth game. It's training for the boss battles ahead, levelling up your skills, connections, and insights.

And here's a pro tip for you: Keep playing the game, even when you've found a comfy spot. Interviewing every 1-2 years isn't just for the career-hungry; it's staying in the loop, vibing with the pulse of the market, and keeping your options as open and endless as your dreams.

Interviewing is like scrolling through the most engaging feeds but in real life. It gives you sneak peeks into industries, trends, and the movers and shakers that define them.

Your generation is known for its passion, creativity, and fearlessness. Apply that in your interviews. Don't just answer questions; ask them.

Don't just fit into roles; shape them. You're not just filling positions; you're defining the future.

So put on your virtual armor or your best real-life outfit, charge fearlessly into those interviews, and know that each one is a step forward, not just in your career, but also in understanding yourself and the world. Keep your passion alive, your curiosity burning, and let every experience mold you into the game-changer you were meant to be. Go rock those interviews, not just for a job but for the sheer thrill of discovery, connection, and growth. Your career is your story, and each interview is a chapter full of adventure, learnings and opportunities.

Finally, remember that on this journey you're not alone. You've got this guide, your own inner strength and a world that's waiting for you.

Stay bold, stay curious and most of all, stay you.

Good luck, and let's see you take the world by storm.

xx

Myrto

Appendix

Online Networking Templates

Below, you'll find five template examples that can serve as a solid starting point for your endeavour to engage in online networking.

These templates are designed to support your interview process while emphasizing the significance of networking.

Template 1: Connecting with an Alumni at the Company

Subject: Seeking Insights for [Position] Role at [Company]

Hi [Name],

I'm a fellow [University] graduate and noticed you're working at [Company], where I have an upcoming interview for the [Position] role. Would you mind sharing a bit about your experience there, especially the company culture and team dynamics? Any insights would be greatly appreciated!

Best,

[Your Name]

Template 2: Reaching out to a Mutual Connection

Subject: Seeking Insights for [Position] Role at [Company]

Hi [Name],

We both know [Mutual Connection], and I saw that you

work at [Company]. I have an interview for the [Position] role and would be grateful to learn more about the company's values and expectations. Could you spare a few minutes to chat?

Thank you,

[Your Name]

Template 3: Approaching Someone in the Same Role or Department

Subject: Seeking Insights for [Position] Role at [Company]

Hi [Name],

I came across your profile while researching [Company] for my upcoming interview for the [Position] role. Your experience and insights into the role and the team could be incredibly helpful for my preparation. Would you have a moment to share some thoughts?

Best regards,

[Your Name]

Template 4: Contacting a Group Member from an Industry-Related Group

Subject: Seeking Insights for [Position] Role at [Company]

Hi [Name],

I noticed we're both members of [LinkedIn Group] and that you work at [Company]. I'm interviewing for a position there soon and would value your perspective on the working environment and any advice you might have for a potential new hire.

Thank you,

[Your Name]

Template 5: Using LinkedIn to Build Your Network

Subject: Connecting with a Fellow [Your University] Graduate

Hi [Name],

I'm a recent graduate from [Your University], and I noticed we share an interest in [Industry/Field]. I'm impressed by your work at [Company] and would love to connect to learn more about your experience. Thank you for considering my request!

Best,

[Your Name]

You can use these templates as a foundation to generate your message and alter it as you see fit. Reach out to your network and gather valuable insights and advice for your upcoming interviews.

Post Interview 'Thank you' Email Templates

Below are some templates examples of thank you notes that you can use to express your gratitude to the interviewers after your interview.

Example 1: Simple and Appreciative

Subject: Thank You for the Interview Opportunity

Dear [Interviewer's Name],

I wanted to extend my heartfelt gratitude for the opportunity to interview for the [Position] role at [Company]. It was a pleasure to learn more about the team and the exciting projects you are working on. I appreciate your time and consideration and look forward to the possibility of contributing to [Company]'s success.

Thank you once again.

Best regards,

[Your Name]

Example 2: Emphasizing Interest and Fit

Subject: Expressing Gratitude for the Interview

Dear [Interviewer's Name],

Thank you for the engaging conversation during my recent interview for the [Position] role at [Company]. I am even more enthusiastic about the potential to contribute to [Company]'s innovative projects and collaborative culture after speaking with you. Your

89

insights into the role have further solidified my interest, and I'm excited about the possibility of joining your team.

Wishing you a great day ahead.

Sincerely,

[Your Name]

Example 3: Reflecting on the Conversation

Subject: Reflecting on Our Conversation

Dear [Interviewer's Name],

I wanted to take a moment to express my gratitude for the enlightening conversation we had during my interview for the [Position] role at [Company]. Your insights into the company's approach to [specific aspect discussed] resonated with me deeply. Thank you for the opportunity to learn more about [Company]'s mission, and I am genuinely excited about the potential to be part of your team.

Warm regards,

[Your Name]

Example 4: Acknowledging the Interview Experience

Subject: Thank You for the Interview Experience

Dear [Interviewer's Name],

I wanted to convey my sincere appreciation for the insightful interview experience I had for the [Position] role at [Company]. The thoughtful questions and the depth of our conversation left a lasting impression on *me. Thank you for taking the time to provide insights into [Company]'s vision and values. I look forward to the chance to contribute to [Company]'s success.*

With gratitude,

[Your Name]

Feel free to adapt these examples to fit your personal style and the specific details of your interview. A thank you note, regardless of the format, is a wonderful way to show appreciation and maintain a positive impression with your interviewers.

Approaching Competency Based and Behavioural Questions

Here I have put together for you, a list of frequent interview questions and tips on how to approach your responses to showcase your skills, values, and experiences effectively.

For each question, you are provided with some Do's and Don'ts, as well as some examples of optimal ways to respond so you can get an idea.

Here's a list of the questions that follow. If you are interested in checking a particular question out flow through the pages, to find the relevant question number.

No	Question
1	Tell us a little bit about yourself
2	Where do you see yourself in five years?
3	Describe a time you made a mistake and how you approached the situation.
4	Describe a situation you handled that didn't bring the expected outcome. Is there something you would do differently now?
5	What can you bring to the role? Why should we hire you?
6	Describe a time of conflict with a colleague and how you approached the situation.
7	Describe a time you solved a problem.
8	Give me an example of a time you demonstrated innovation or changed an existing process.
9	What are your strengths?
10	What are your weaknesses?

11	Describe a time when you had to manage conflict with a manager. How did you handle it?
12	How did you respond to a task assigned to you, that was against your values
13	Tell me about a time you missed a deadline.
14	Tell me about a time you had to deliver a project with tight deadlines.
15	Describe a situation where you had to work with a difficult team member. How did you handle it?
16	Tell me about a time when you had to adapt to significant changes at work.
17	Describe how you prioritize your tasks when faced with multiple tight deadlines.
18	Tell me about a time you took the lead on a project. What was the outcome?
19	Tell me about a time you took the lead on a project. What was the outcome?
20	What are your salary expectations?
21	Do you have any other interviews lined up?

QUESTION 1: Tell us a little bit about yourself.

Do

- Begin with a brief overview of your professional background.
- Highlight key skills and experiences relevant to the position.
- Conclude with a statement on why you're interested in the role or how your personal passions align with the company's mission.

Don't

- Go into a detailed personal history that doesn't relate to the job.
- Speak too long; keep it concise and to the point.
- Be overly generic without giving specifics about your career or your alignment with the role.

Example 1: "I recently graduated with a degree in computer science, where I focused on machine learning. During my studies, I interned at a tech startup, working on optimizing algorithms. I was also active in our university's coding club, leading workshops for new members. I'm passionate about using technology to solve real-world problems, and I'm excited about the opportunity to bring my skills and enthusiasm to your team."

Example 2: "With a background in marketing and communications, I've just completed my degree, focusing on digital marketing strategies. During college, I volunteered to manage social media for a local non-profit, increasing their online engagement by 40%. I've also completed a summer internship with an advertising agency, where I assisted in campaign development. I'm drawn to your organization's innovative approach to marketing and believe I can contribute fresh ideas and energy to your team."

Example 3: "As a seasoned sales professional in the pharmaceutical industry, I've consistently achieved and surpassed sales targets by cultivating strong relationships with clients and understanding their unique needs. My blend of analytical thinking and personable communication skills has enabled me to excel in competitive markets. I am thrilled at the prospect of bringing these strengths to your dynamic team and contributing to your growth goals."

By focusing on your professional experiences, key skills, and alignment with the role, you can provide a concise yet impactful answer to this question. Make sure to tailor your response to reflect the specific role and organisation to make it as relevant, as possible.

QUESTION 2: Where do you see yourself in five years?

Do

- Reflect on your aspirations and future plans.
- Align your answer with the company's goals and demonstrate your commitment to growth.
- Show enthusiasm for long-term engagement and development within the organization.

Don't

- Mention plans that indicate a lack of dedication to the role or company.
- Provide vague or unrealistic goals that are unrelated to the position.

Example 1: "In five years, I hope to have grown within your organization, taking on more responsibilities and contributing to key projects. I'm keen on enhancing my skills in project management and leadership, possibly leading a small team. I see myself becoming an integral part of your company, driving innovative solutions and helping shape the future direction of our products."

Example 2: "Five years from now, I envision myself as a specialist in data analytics, utilizing my mathematical background to provide insights and drive decision-making. I'm committed to continuous learning, pursuing certifications, and attending workshops that align with your company's mission. I'm excited about the opportunity to contribute and grow within a collaborative and forward-thinking environment."

Example 3: "In five years, I see myself contributing to the field of sustainable energy, potentially managing projects that align with the company's goals of environmental stewardship. I plan to deepen my expertise by attending industry conferences, networking with professionals, and seeking mentorship within the organization. I believe that my passion for sustainability, coupled with my commitment to professional growth, aligns perfectly with your company's values and long-term vision.

This approach emphasizes alignment with the company's vision, commitment to growth, and focus on realistic and actionable plans. It reflects the perspective of early career professionals and recent graduates, balancing aspiration with attainability.

QUESTION 3: Describe a time you made a mistake and how you approached the situation.

Do

- Select a relevant mistake that allowed for personal or professional growth.
- Demonstrate your ability to take responsibility, correct the mistake, and learn from the experience.
- Emphasize problem-solving, communication, and positive outcomes.

Don't

- Pick a trivial or irrelevant mistake.
- Place blame on others or make excuses for the mistake.
- Claim that you never make mistakes or provide an overly rehearsed answer.

Example 1: "During my internship, I made an error in a data entry task that caused inaccuracies in a report. I immediately realized my mistake and informed my supervisor. Together, we corrected the data, and I then took the initiative to create a verification process to prevent similar errors in the future. This mistake taught me the importance of double-checking my work and not being afraid to seek help when needed."

Example 2: "While working on a group project in college, I misunderstood an assignment deadline, which caused a delay in our submission. I openly acknowledged my mistake to the team, and we worked together to complete the project as quickly as possible. I learned the importance of clear communication and paying close attention to details. I have since implemented better organizational tools and habits to ensure I stay on top of deadlines."

Example 3: "In my first job after graduation, I made an error in a marketing campaign, using outdated information in a customer email blast. When I realized the mistake, I immediately notified my manager and worked with the team to send a corrected email. I also proposed a new process for verifying information before sending out future communications. This experience taught me the value of owning my mistakes and proactively finding solutions to prevent them from happening again."

These examples reflect situations that early career professionals and recent graduates might encounter. They emphasize responsibility, learning, and growth from mistakes, reinforcing an understanding of the importance of these attributes in a professional setting.

QUESTION 4: Describe a situation you handled that didn't bring the expected outcome. Is there something you would do differently now?

Do

- Select a situation that was challenging but also provided an opportunity for growth and learning.
- Describe what you did to try to remedy the situation and what you learned from the experience.
- Talk about what you would do differently now, reflecting on your growth and increased understanding.

Don't

- Choose an example that portrays you in an entirely negative or irresponsible light.
- Place blame solely on external factors or other people.
- Convey that you learned nothing from the situation or wouldn't make any changes in your approach.

Example 1: "During my senior design project, our team planned a specific method for completing the project but ended up missing our deadline. Despite our efforts to correct course, we didn't achieve the result we wanted. Looking back, I realize we lacked a clear communication plan and didn't seek feedback early enough. If I faced this situation again, I would set regular check-ins with team members and advisors to ensure alignment and catch potential issues earlier."

Example 2: "In my first sales role, I worked diligently on a proposal for a potential client. Despite my best efforts, the client chose a competitor's offer. I realized later that I didn't fully understand the client's specific needs and focused too much on our standard offerings. Now, I would take more time to listen to the client and tailor our solution to their unique challenges and goals, enhancing the value proposition."

Example 3: "During a college internship, I was tasked with organizing an event to promote our company's services. Unfortunately, the turnout was lower than expected. Reflecting on it, I see that our promotional efforts were too general and didn't reach our target audience effectively. If I were to do it again, I would utilize more targeted marketing channels and collaborate with local partners to boost visibility and engagement."

These examples emphasize the learning process and self-improvement, demonstrating an ability to analyse situations critically and apply lessons learned. They also showcase adaptability and resilience, valuable traits for recent graduates and those early in their careers.

QUESTION 5: What can you bring to the role? Why should we hire you?

Do

- Clearly articulate your unique strengths, skills, and qualities that align with the role.
- Demonstrate your understanding of the company and its goals.
- Show enthusiasm and passion for the role and the industry.
- Provide specific examples or experiences that illustrate your suitability for the position.

Don't

- Give generic or vague answers that could apply to anyone.
- Oversell yourself to the point where it seems unrealistic.
- Fail to provide any concrete reasons or examples.
- Neglect to research the company, role, or industry.

Example 1: "With my recent degree in marketing and hands-on experience in social media campaigns during my internship, I can bring fresh and innovative strategies to your team. My ability to analyse consumer trends aligns with your company's mission to create customer-centric campaigns. My passion for creative storytelling will help me engage your target audience effectively."

Example 2: "I believe my background in computer science, coupled with my experience in team projects and hackathons, makes me an excellent fit for this software development role. I have practical experience in using Agile methodologies and am adept at problem-solving, which I demonstrated by developing a solution for a complex problem during my senior project. I am eager to contribute my technical skills and collaborative mindset to your team."

Example 3: "As a recent graduate in environmental science, I have a solid foundation in sustainability practices, which aligns with your company's commitment to eco-friendly initiatives. During my summer research, I was part of a project that reduced water consumption in local agriculture by implementing new irrigation techniques. I can bring this analytical approach and passion for environmental stewardship to your sustainability team."

These examples provide a blend of education, experience, passion, and alignment with the company's goals and values. Tailoring the response to the specific role and showing how one's unique background will be an asset can help recent graduates and early-career professionals stand out in their response to this question.

QUESTION 6: Describe a time of conflict with a colleague and how you approached the situation.

Do

- Provide a real example, focusing on the situation, the conflict, and the resolution.
- Emphasize your role in finding a solution, highlighting your communication and teamwork skills.
- Reflect on what you learned from the experience and how it helped you grow.

Don't

- Speak negatively about the colleague or blame others.
- Choose a trivial or irrelevant example that doesn't showcase your problem-solving or interpersonal skills.
- Exaggerate the situation or your role in resolving it.
- Avoid answering the question or give a vague response.

Example 1: "During a group project at university, my team had different opinions on how to approach the assignment. One team member wanted to take a direction I strongly disagreed with. Instead of arguing, I suggested a team meeting where we openly discussed our ideas. We found a compromise that blended our strategies, and the project was successful. It taught me the value of open communication and collaboration."

Example 2: "In my first job, I faced a conflict with a colleague over prioritizing tasks for a shared project. We both had strong opinions but were struggling to find common ground. I decided to schedule a one-on-one meeting to understand his perspective better. By listening to each other's concerns and finding the overlapping interests, we managed to agree on a shared plan. This experience reinforced my belief in constructive dialogue as a tool for resolving conflicts."

Example 3: "During an internship, I had a disagreement with a colleague about the design approach for a client proposal. We were both passionate about our ideas but seemed to be at a standstill. I took the initiative to break down both our concepts and find the strengths and weaknesses in each. By focusing on the project's goals rather than our individual preferences, we were able to create a hybrid solution that pleased both us and the client. It was a valuable lesson in putting the team's needs above personal preferences."

These examples highlight the importance of communication, collaboration, empathy, and putting the team or project's needs first. By focusing on how the conflict was resolved rather than dwelling on the disagreement, you show potential employers your ability to work effectively with others, even when conflicts arise.

QUESTION 7: Describe a time you solved a problem.

Do

- Identify a relevant and specific problem that you were instrumental in solving.
- Describe the process of how you approached and solved the problem, highlighting your problem-solving and critical-thinking skills.
- Share the positive outcome and any lessons you learned that demonstrate growth and adaptability.

Don't

- Be too vague or general in describing the problem and solution.
- Focus on a problem that doesn't highlight your skills or relevant attributes.
- Overstate your role in solving the problem or take credit for others' work.

Example 1: "During my final semester at university, I noticed that the study group I was a part of was struggling to coordinate meeting times. I created a shared online calendar where everyone could input their availability. By visualizing our schedules, we quickly found suitable meeting times and improved our collaboration. It taught me that even simple technological solutions can greatly enhance teamwork."

Example 2: "In my first role as a junior analyst, I identified a recurring error in our data reporting process that was affecting the accuracy of the reports. I took the initiative to investigate the issue and discovered an inconsistency in how data was being entered. I proposed a standardized method and created a guide to ensure uniform data entry. Implementing this change improved the accuracy of our reports and streamlined our process."

Example 3: "During my internship, I was assigned to a project that was behind schedule due to unexpected challenges. I analysed the existing workflow and identified bottlenecks that were causing delays. I proposed a revised plan that reallocated resources and included contingency steps. The project was completed on time, and my approach was later adopted for other projects. This experience taught me the importance of proactive analysis and flexibility in project management."

These examples focus on different types of problems - logistical, technical, and project-related - and demonstrate how identifying the root cause and taking initiative can lead to successful resolutions. By emphasizing the process and the positive outcome, you can illustrate your adaptability, creativity, and problem-solving skills, which are valuable traits for any role.

QUESTION 8: Give me an example of a time you demonstrated innovation or changed an existing process.

Do

- Select an instance where you identified an opportunity for improvement and took action.

- Detail the specific problem, your innovative approach or solution, and the positive impact it had.
- Emphasize how your creativity, critical thinking, or ability to see things from a different perspective led to the change.

Don't

- Choose an example that doesn't directly relate to innovation or change in a process.
- Speak in overly technical terms if it's not necessary for the context of the role.
- Fail to include the impact of your innovative change or gloss over the specific steps you took.

Example 1: "While working on a group project during college, I noticed that we were spending a lot of time on repetitive tasks. I developed a simple automation script that cut our workload in half, allowing us to focus on more critical aspects of the project. This not only improved our efficiency but also enhanced the overall quality of our work."

Example 2: "In my role as a junior developer at Company X, I identified a flaw in our code review process that was leading to delays. I proposed a new peer review system that allowed for continuous feedback and incorporated automated testing. This reduced the time required for code reviews by 30% and fostered a more collaborative environment."

Example 3: "During my internship at a non-profit

organization, I realized that our outreach efforts to potential donors were fragmented and inconsistent. I took the initiative to redesign the process by implementing a centralized database and creating a consistent communication strategy. This streamlined our outreach efforts and resulted in a 20% increase in donor engagement."

These examples show how an innovative approach doesn't necessarily mean inventing something entirely new; it can be about seeing an existing process from a different angle and finding ways to make it more effective or efficient. By focusing on a real-world scenario where you applied creativity, critical thinking, and problem-solving, you demonstrate your ability to bring valuable innovative thinking to the role.

QUESTION 9: What are your strengths?

Do

- Identify specific strengths that align with the role you're applying for.
- Provide examples or evidence of how you've demonstrated these strengths in your studies, internships, or early career experiences.
- Reflect on how these strengths will contribute to your success in the role.

Don't

- List generic strengths without providing context or examples.
- Overstate your abilities or claim strengths that

don't genuinely apply to you.

- Focus solely on strengths that aren't relevant to the role.

Example 1: "One of my strengths is my ability to communicate effectively. During my university group projects, I often took on the role of spokesperson because of my comfort in articulating our ideas. I believe this strength will be invaluable in client-facing roles, where clear communication is key."

Example 2: "I pride myself on my analytical thinking. In my recent internship with Company XYZ, I applied my analytical skills to analyse market trends, and my insights contributed to a 15% increase in sales over the quarter. This ability to assess and interpret data will help me contribute positively to your team."

Example 3: "My strength in problem-solving was tested when I was working on a software project that had a tight deadline. Despite encountering unexpected issues, I was able to find creative solutions without compromising the quality. This demonstrated my resilience and adaptability, qualities I'll carry into this new role."

By focusing on strengths that directly align with the job description and providing tangible examples from your early career or academic experiences, you can construct an answer that not only highlights your personal abilities but also underscores why those strengths make you a strong candidate for the position.

QUESTION 10: What are your weaknesses?

Do

- Select a genuine weakness that you're working to improve.
- Explain the steps you've taken or are planning to take to overcome this weakness.
- Connect it to a learning experience or growth opportunity, rather than a failure.

Don't

- Choose a weakness that is a core requirement for the role.
- Disguise a strength as a weakness (e.g., "I work too hard").
- Simply state a weakness without explaining how you are addressing it.

Example 1: "One of my weaknesses has been time management. During my first semester at university, I found myself overwhelmed with my studies. Since then, I've started using planning tools and setting specific goals, and I've noticed a significant improvement in my ability to meet deadlines. I'm continually working on this skill to ensure I manage my time efficiently."

Example 2: "I've struggled with public speaking in the past, feeling nervous when presenting in front of large groups. Recognizing this, I enrolled in a public speaking course and actively sought opportunities to present in my classes. Although it's still a work in progress, I've become much more comfortable and confident in my abilities."

Example 3: "In the early stages of my internship, I realized that I was hesitant to ask for help when I needed it. I've learned that collaboration and seeking guidance when necessary is vital, and I've been working on being more open and communicative with my colleagues. It's an ongoing process, but I'm committed to improving in this area."

By focusing on self-awareness, demonstrating a commitment to personal growth, and aligning your response with experiences relevant to early careers or recent graduates, you can present your weaknesses in a way that shows maturity, responsibility, and a readiness to take on professional challenges.

QUESTION 11: Describe a time when you had to manage conflict with a manager. How did you handle it?

Do

- Focus on a real situation where you faced a disagreement or misunderstanding with a manager.
- Emphasize the respectful and professional way, you addressed the issue.
- Highlight your problem-solving skills, communication abilities, and willingness to work collaboratively.

Don't

- Exaggerate or fabricate a conflict.
- Speak negatively or unprofessionally about the manager or company.
- Present yourself as confrontational or unwilling to consider other perspectives.

Example 1: *"During my internship, I was assigned a project that had unclear expectations. When I discussed it with my manager, we had different understandings of what was required. I handled it by scheduling a one-on-one meeting where we clearly outlined the project's goals and my responsibilities. This open communication helped us align our expectations, and the project was completed successfully."*

Example 2: *"While working on a group project at university, I disagreed with my supervisor's approach to a particular problem. I took the time to research alternative solutions and presented my findings in a respectful manner. Though my approach wasn't ultimately chosen, my supervisor appreciated my initiative and the way I communicated my perspective."*

Example 3: *"In my part-time job, I faced a scheduling conflict that clashed with my study commitments. I approached my manager calmly and presented my situation, offering alternative solutions to ensure my responsibilities were covered. My manager appreciated my proactive approach, and we were able to find a solution that met both our needs."*

By focusing on positive communication,

collaboration, and an understanding of the broader context, your response can demonstrate your ability to handle conflicts with a manager professionally and constructively. These examples provide a way for early career individuals and recent graduates to showcase their maturity and problem-solving abilities.

QUESTION 12: How did you respond to a task assigned to you, that was against your values?

Do

- Explain the specific ethical dilemma.
- Emphasize your values and how you upheld them.
- Share the solution and how it aligned with both your values and the organization's needs.

Don't

- Criticize or blame others.
- Use an example that might portray you in an extremely negative light.

Example 1: "I was once asked to promote a product that I knew had questionable quality. I expressed my concerns to my supervisor and proposed an alternative approach to improve the product before launching the marketing campaign. This aligned with my values of integrity and honesty."

Example 2: "When faced with a task that conflicted with my values, I engaged in a transparent dialogue with my team to express my reservations.

Together, we found a solution that upheld the company's ethics and satisfied the project's requirements."

QUESTION 13: Tell me about a time you missed a deadline.

Do

- Acknowledge the missed deadline.
- Explain the actions you took to rectify the situation.
- Highlight what you learned and the steps to avoid future occurrences.

Don't

- Blame others or external factors solely.
- Downplay the seriousness of missing a deadline.

Example 1: "I missed a deadline for a deliverable due to unexpected technical issues. I promptly communicated with the stakeholders, worked extra hours to complete the task, and implemented additional checks to prevent future delays."

Example 2: "I once missed a deadline due to miscommunication within the team. I took responsibility, coordinated with the team to expedite the work, and introduced regular progress checks to ensure alignment and timely completion in the future."

QUESTION 14: Tell me about a time you had to

deliver a project with tight deadlines.

Do

- Describe how you managed your time and resources.
- Emphasize your ability to work under pressure.
- Highlight successful outcomes and teamwork.

Don't

- Focus on the stress or negative aspects of the situation.
- Provide vague or general responses without specific examples.

Example 1: "I was assigned a project with a tight two-week deadline. I quickly developed a comprehensive plan, engaged the team in a focused effort, and utilized all available resources. Through collaboration and efficient management, we delivered the project on time and met the client's expectations."

Example 2: "In a fast-paced environment, I led a team to complete a complex project within a tight timeframe. We held daily stand-up meetings, prioritized tasks, and worked closely with all stakeholders to ensure alignment. Despite the challenges, we delivered a high-quality project on time, enhancing our reputation with the client."

QUESTION 15: 'Describe a situation where you had to work with a difficult team member. How did you handle it?

Do

- Focus on your actions to resolve the situation.
- Highlight communication and understanding.
- Emphasize positive outcomes.

Don't

- Speak negatively about the team member.
- Ignore the importance of teamwork.

Example 1: "I worked with a team member who often missed deadlines. I approached them privately to understand the underlying issues and offered assistance. We established clear expectations, and their performance improved, benefiting the entire team."

Example 2: "A team member was reluctant to share information, causing confusion. I facilitated open discussions and team-building activities, encouraging collaboration and trust. This ultimately led to a more cohesive and effective team."

QUESTION 16: Tell me about a time when you had to adapt to significant changes at work.

Do

- Describe the change and its impact.
- Emphasize your flexibility and positive attitude.
- Highlight the results and what you learned.

Don't

- Resist or minimize the significance of the change.
- Focus solely on negative aspects.

Example 1: "When our company merged with a competitor, I took the initiative to understand the new procedures and actively engaged with new colleagues. My adaptability helped smooth the transition and strengthened interdepartmental relationships."

Example 2: "Our organization shifted to remote work unexpectedly. I quickly adapted my team's workflow, implementing new communication tools and regular check-ins, ensuring productivity and maintaining team morale during the transition."

QUESTION 17: Describe how you prioritize your tasks when faced with multiple tight deadlines.

Do

- Explain your method for prioritization.
- Highlight tools or strategies you use.
- Show how your approach leads to success.

Don't

- Provide a vague or overly simplistic answer.
- Ignore the importance of communication with stakeholders.

Example 1: "Faced with multiple deadlines, I create a detailed timeline and prioritize tasks based on urgency and importance. Regular communication with stakeholders helps me adjust as needed, ensuring that critical tasks are completed on time."

Example 2: "When handling several tight deadlines, I use project management tools to visualize and organize tasks. Collaborating with team members to delegate and align on priorities ensures that we meet all deadlines without sacrificing quality."

QUESTION 18: Tell me about a time you took the lead on a project. What was the outcome?

Do

- Describe the project and your role as a leader.
- Emphasize teamwork, leadership skills, and achievements.
- Highlight the positive outcome and learning

experiences.

Don't

- Overlook the contributions of others.
- Focus only on successes without acknowledging learning opportunities.

Example 1: "I led a cross-functional team on a key project, implementing clear goals and regular progress checks. My leadership fostered collaboration and accountability, leading to the project's completion ahead of schedule and under budget."

Example 2: "Taking the lead on a challenging initiative, I engaged the team through transparent communication and encouragement. Although we faced hurdles, our collective efforts led to a successful outcome, and I learned valuable insights into managing diverse talents and expectations."

QUESTION 19: Can you explain this gap on your CV?

Do

- Be Honest. Explain the gap truthfully without going into unnecessary details.
- Focus on the positive. Share what you learned or achieved during that time, even if it wasn't directly related to your career.
- Emphasize your readiness. Highlight how the gap has prepared you for the role you're seeking now.

Don't

- Avoid negative language or speaking negatively about past employers or yourself.
- Don't over-explain. Keep your explanation brief and focused; going into too much detail might raise more questions.

Examples 1: Gap due to job search difficulty (Recent Graduate)

"After graduating, I took some time to explore various career paths and find the right fit for my skills and interests. While it took longer than anticipated, I used that time to volunteer in my community and further develop my skills in [specific area]. I'm now more confident about the direction I want to take and believe this role aligns perfectly with my career goals."

Example 2: Gap due to layoff

"I was part of a company-wide layoff, which, while unexpected, gave me an opportunity to reflect on my career and invest in my personal growth. I took online courses in [specific skills], volunteered, and engaged in freelance projects to stay sharp. I believe these experiences have prepared me well for the challenges of the [Position Name] role."

Example 3: Gap for personal development or other reasons

"During that time, I focused on personal development and honing skills that are relevant to my career goals. I took courses in [specific area], worked on personal projects, and engaged with my professional network. I see that time as an investment in myself and my career, and I believe I'm now well-prepared for this opportunity."

Example 4: Gap due to family care responsibilities

"After a family member fell ill, I made the decision to take some time off to provide care and support. While it was a challenging period, it reinforced my values and taught me skills like time management, empathy, and resilience. During that time, I also kept up with industry trends and took online courses to continue developing my professional skills. I'm now ready to return to the workforce, and I'm excited about the opportunity to bring my enhanced skills and perspective to the [Position Name] role at [Company Name]."

Example 5: Gap due to caring for children

"I took some time off to focus on my family and raise my children during their early years. This period was invaluable in developing skills such as multitasking, organization, time management, and patience. While I was dedicated to my family, I also

stayed connected to my industry by [mention any relevant activities, such as reading industry publications, attending workshops, or part-time work]. I'm now eager to return to my career, and I believe the [Position Name] role at [Company Name] aligns perfectly with my skills and aspirations."

Example 6: Gap due to Military service

"During that period, I fulfilled my obligations to serve in the army. This experience was instrumental in developing key skills such as leadership, teamwork, discipline, and adaptability. I also had the opportunity to work in situations that required problem-solving and strategic thinking. Though it was a departure from my civilian career path, I believe the skills and experiences I gained during my service have enriched my professional profile and make me a strong candidate for the [Position Name] role at [Company Name].

QUESTION 20: What are your salary expectations?

Do

- Do your research, know the typical salary range for the role in your location and industry.
- Be honest and share a realistic figure based on your qualifications, experience, and the industry standard.

- Consider the entire package. Keep in mind that compensation isn't just salary; benefits, bonuses, and other perks can be part of the negotiation.

Don't

- Be too specific too soon. If you can, try to understand more about the role and responsibilities before naming a specific figure.
- Sell yourself short. Be confident in your value, and don't immediately accept an offer below your worth.
- Make it only about money. While salary is important, convey that it's not the only factor in your decision.

Example 1: If you want to understand the role better before giving a specific figure:

"I would like to learn more about the specific responsibilities and expectations of the role to provide an accurate salary expectation. Could you provide more details about the role or perhaps share the salary range budgeted for this position?"

Example 2: If you have a specific range in mind

"Based on my research and understanding of the role, my expectations would be in the range of \$[X] to \$[Y]. However, I'm open to discussing the entire compensation package, including benefits and growth opportunities."

Example 3: If You Want to Defer the Question to a Later Stage

"I'm primarily focused on finding a position that's the right fit for my career goals. I'm confident that if we determine I'm the right person for this role, we can come to a mutually acceptable compensation arrangement. Could we revisit this later in the process?"

Remember, it's important to approach the salary question with confidence and a clear understanding of your value and the market rate for the position. How and when you choose to discuss specific figures may vary depending on the stage of the interview process and the context of the conversation.

QUESTION 21: Do you have any other interviews lined up?

Do

- Be honest and answer truthfully about whether you have other interviews. Honesty is always the best policy.
- Emphasize your genuine interest in the company you're interviewing with.
- Express enthusiasm for the position and the company's values, culture, and mission.
- Explain why you see yourself as a good fit for the company and how your skills align with their needs.
- Share how you can contribute to the company's success and growth.
- Maintain a professional and positive tone in your response.
- If you have other interviews, let them know

you are committed to progressing through the interview process responsibly.

- Acknowledge that you're considering multiple opportunities but convey your respect for the interview process with each company.

Don't

- Lie about having other interviews, as it could damage your credibility.
- Avoid sharing unnecessary details about the specific companies or positions you're interviewing for.
- Don't imply that other opportunities are better or that you're not genuinely interested in the current company.
- Refrain from boasting about the number of interviews you have or using it to appear in demand.

Your response should reflect your enthusiasm for the company you're interviewing with while being respectful of your other opportunities. It's about striking a balance between showcasing your interest and being professional in your approach.

All these examples shared above, can be adapted or expanded based on specific needs of the role you are interviewing for or the general context.

Questions for the interviewers

Here's a few examples of questions you can get inspiration from and use them as your questions towards the end of the interview.

You will find the questions grouped, in different categories based on their theme and focus.

It would be great to have 2-3 questions in mind, ahead of you interview and ideally from different categories.

Understanding the Role and Team

1. "Can you describe the most important projects that this role will be involved in over the next year?"
2. "How does this position fit into the larger team structure, and how does it contribute to the organization's success?"
3. "What are the most common career paths for individuals who have been in this position?"

Aligning with Company Values and Culture

1. "How does the company put its values into practice on a daily basis?"
2. "Can you share an example of a recent company decision that reflects its core values?"
3. "What initiatives does the organization have in place to foster diversity and inclusion?"

Focusing on Growth and Development

1. "How does the company support ongoing professional development and continuous learning?"
2. "What opportunities will I have to collaborate with different departments or teams?"
3. "Can you tell me about a recent success story within the team, and what it took to get there?"

Demonstrating Thoughtfulness - Strategic Thinking

1. "What are the most significant challenges currently facing the team, and how is the company addressing them?"
2. "How does the organization stay ahead of the competition in [specific area relevant to the industry]?"
3. "Can you share how the company's strategy has evolved in response to industry trends or changes?"

Expressing Interest in Contributing

1. "How can the person in this role make a meaningful impact in the first 90 days?"
2. "What does success look like for this position, and how is it measured?"
3. "How does the team celebrate successes, and how does it learn from failures?"

Encouraging a Two-Way Conversation

1. "What do you enjoy most and least about

working here, and what makes this company unique?"

2. "Is there anything about my background or experience that you would like me to expand upon?"

3. "What qualities or experiences do you believe would make someone exceptional in this role?"

These questions are tailored to convey curiosity, engagement, alignment with the company's mission, and a focus on growth and collaboration. They should help you make a strong impression and stand out as a thoughtful and interested candidate. Feel free to adapt them to fit the specific role, company, and industry you are interviewing for every time.

During the time you have to ask questions, you may also want to understand more about the hiring manager if they are part of the interview. Understanding how a line manager supports development and fosters psychological safety is essential.

Questions to gauge the Line Manager's approach

Regarding Professional Development and Support

1. "How do you, as a manager, support your team's professional growth and development?"
2. "Can you describe any mentorship or coaching programs within the team?"
3. "How do you work with team members to set and track professional development goals?"
4. "What resources and opportunities are available for continuing education or skill-building?"
5. "How do you encourage team members to explore new ideas or take on new challenges?"

Regarding Psychological Safety and Team Culture

1. "How do you foster a culture of trust and open communication within the team?"
2. "Can you share an example of how you've handled a situation where a team member made a mistake or faced a failure?"
3. "What measures are in place to ensure that team members feel comfortable expressing their thoughts, concerns, or innovative ideas?"
4. "How do you facilitate constructive feedback within the team, and how are conflicts resolved?"
5. "What values or principles guide your leadership style, especially in ensuring psychological safety and well-being?"
6. "How does the team celebrate diversity of

thought, and how are different perspectives encouraged?"

These questions focus on the manager's approach to professional development, collaboration, trust-building, and creating a safe and inclusive environment. The answers can provide valuable insights into whether this is a manager and team where you would thrive and feel supported in your growth and well-being.

Want to keep the conversation going?

I would love to connect with you and continue sharing, insights, updates and career advice.

You can find me on LinkedIn www.linkedin.com/in/myrto-skourletou, or Instagram & Tiktok @graduatecareer, where I regularly post content to inspire and assist you on your career journey.

Let's keep learning and growing together.

See you online!

Printed in Great Britain
by Amazon

27168967R00079